THE MANUAL
OF PUBLIC SPEAKING

THE MANUAL
OF PUBLIC SPEAKING

*A Guide for the
Chairman, Secretary and Club Official,
The Business Man, Trade Unionist, and
Political Aspirant.*

By
PATRICK PRINGLE

*How to Speak in Public
Examples of Model Speeches
Voice Production and Elocution*

LONDON
W. FOULSHAM & CO. LTD
NEW YORK · TORONTO · CAPE TOWN · SYDNEY

W. FOULSHAM & Co. Ltd.,
Yeovil Road, Slough, Bucks, England.

Lornas
Book

ISBN-0-572-00012-X

Printed in England by
Hillman Printers (Frome) Limited, Somerset

CONTENTS

PREFACE

WE live in an age of committees and conferences, and ordinary men and women are called upon to play increasingly large parts in the conduct of meetings of many different kinds. Some people enjoy these activities: others regard them with dismay and fear. All need to know what to do.

For knowledge is power, and the main cause of fear is ignorance. A person may be horrified at being asked to express his opinions to a meeting, even if he knows everyone there personally and perhaps has just been airing his views to as many as would listen to him at the bar. He will probably be even more alarmed if he is asked to take the chair. In each case his fear is of making a fool of himself through not knowing what he ought to do.

Persons meet for a great variety of purposes, but the conduct of all meetings is based on certain general principles. The purpose of this book is to say what these are and to show how they should be followed. Most bodies that hold meetings have their own particular regulations, but generally there is little procedural difference between speaking or taking the chair at a company meeting or an Old Boys' reunion —between discussing working conditions at a trade union branch meeting and bar prices at a meeting of the local tennis club.

CHAPTER I

ELECTING A CHAIRMAN

As civilization progresses, so the business of the people is conducted more and more by means of meetings. To-day we have reached a point when thousands of meetings are held annually in every town and city of the country. Some are important affairs, called to deliberate on vital matters affecting a whole community, while others are merely gatherings that concern the working of some small social club.

No matter what the size or importance of the gathering, it must be ruled and guided by a chairman, if it is to be conducted on orderly lines. Thus, the first thing when a meeting is to be held is for it to be in possession of a chairman.

It will be recognised that when a society, a club or any other body is about to appoint its chairman, the procedure will vary according to whether or not a chairman already exists. In the case of a gathering that meets for the first time, no such official will exist, and the methods to be applied will not be exactly the same as those used in appointing a chairman to replace one already in office.

APPOINTING THE FIRST CHAIRMAN.—When a body meets for the first time, or when it only has to meet

once to fulfil its duties, those responsbile for conven-
ing the meeting must set the business in motion.
Usually, one of these people will rise and say, " I
propose that Mr. A. be nominated as chairman."
Immediately, a friend of the proposer stands and says,
" I second that."

One of two things now happens. Usually, those
who are present, being anxious to get on with the
business, intimate their assent by crying " agreed," by
holding up their hands, or by any other method that
occurs to them. This settles the matter and, on a
unanimous vote, Mr. A. becomes the chairman.

Some of the conveners now come forward and escort
Mr. A. to the chair. Once installed there, Mr. A.
expresses his thanks in a few chosen words and says
that he will carry out the trust reposed in him to the
best of his ability. He then turns to the real business
in hand.

APPOINTING A TEMPORARY CHAIRMAN.—But, it
sometimes happens that the first step does not proceed
as smoothly as we have suggested. There may be rival
parties or people present who have " axes to grind "
and who are not prepared to accept Mr. A. as their
chairman.

When unanimity does not exist, there is only one
course, and that is for one of the conveners of the
meeting to propose Mr. A. as the temporary chairman,
using the method already indicated for the purpose.
On someone seconding this proposal, Mr. A. takes the
chair temporarily. He does not proceed with the actual
business of the meeting, but deals with the election

of a real chairman and vacates his position the moment the voting has determined this official.

There is absolutely no sense in anyone obstructing the appointment of a temporary chairman, since it assists all parties to get on with the business. Thus, there need be no fear that this method may be inadequate to meet even the most awkward situation.

THE TEMPORARY CHAIRMAN'S DUTIES.—Once installed in the chair, the temporary chairman rises and says, " Ladies and Gentlemen, I shall now be glad to receive nominations for the post of chairman." He may also intimate that a time limit is to be put on every speaker, alleging as his reason that much important business must be gone through and time is short. A reasonable allowance is three minutes.

Usually, somebody will jump up and say, " I propose that Mr. B. be nominated for the chair." This person will probably continue by setting out Mr. B.'s qualifications which fit him for the post. The whole of this speaker's remarks must be limited to three minutes' duration or whatever time has been selected by the temporary chairman.

As soon as the speaker sits down, one of his supporters may be calculated to rise and say, " I would like to second that proposal (or nomination)."

There is now one name before the meeting and others may follow in exactly the same way. When no more are forthcoming, the temporary chairman puts all the names before the gathering and they are voted upon.

The voting may be done in any reasonable way: the usual method is by a show of hands. Each candidate is voted on in turn, usually in the order in which they were proposed or in alphabetical order. The number of votes cast for each is recorded, and if no nomination is carried the candidate who has received the largest number of votes may be considered elected. A fairer method is to eliminate the candidate who received the smallest number of votes and then vote on all the others again. If there is still no absolute majority, the candidate with the next lowest number of votes may be eliminated, and this process can be continued until a nomination is carried.

It is illegal for anyone to preside at his own election, so the temporary chairman cannot be elected permanent chairman. In other words, no one who is likely to be chosen permanent chairman should take the chair for the election.

There is nothing to stop a person from proposing, seconding, or voting for himself as chairman, although all these courses may well be inadvisable.

ELECTING CHAIRMEN PERIODICALLY.—Most bodies, societies, companies, etc., elect their chairmen for a given period of time, which period can, as a rule, be renewed on its expiry. The period is stated in the rules, by-laws, etc., of the concern. When a fresh chairman is to be elected, the fact should be stated on the agenda of the meeting. At the meeting, it is the sitting chairman who directs the election, exactly as described already under the heading of " The Temporary Chairman's Duties."

ABSENCE OF THE CHAIRMAN.—Should the chairman be absent from a meeting, his place is taken by the vice-chairman if there is one. If there is not, a temporary chairman may be elected for the occasion.

When only one name is submitted, it must be put to the vote in exactly the same way as if there were several. The fact that there is no opposition and that the wishes of the meeting are clear is not in itself sufficient. The name must be put to the vote.

CHAPTER II

SOME people are born chairmen. They have exactly the right temperament for the office and they know just how to proceed in any circumstance. But many are not so favourably gifted ; yet it often happens that those who are less favoured may possess some peculiar knowledge which makes it imperative that they should take up the office. Accordingly, it is not at all rare to find a man or woman seated in the chair who feels very much out of place in that important position.

As this book is written primarily for the individual who allows himself to be elected to the chair more as a sense of duty than from a love of power, we will begin by supposing that you have attended a meeting and, somewhat to your surprise, you find that it is the will of those present that you should take the chair.

Probably, your first inclinations will be to reject the honour which the meeting wishes to confer on you, and you will set about hiding your light under a bushel. This is a very natural attitude on your part, and it speaks well for your modesty ; but it is not a line of action in which you should persist. After the first shock of finding yourself in the centre of the limelight, your duty is to pull yourself together and accept the honour graciously. After all, every chairman, even the most gifted, had to make a start at some time or other and, unless you belong to the very nervous type of person, there is no reason at all why you should not make a complete success of the office when you have once thrown yourself into the work.

THE NECESSARY QUALITIES OF A CHAIRMAN.—The primary duty of a chairman is to control and guide the meeting. Where a number of people are gathered together, it is only reasonable to suppose that many divergent views will exist. Some will want one thing, some another. Some will express themselves in a friendly manner, others will become heated and aggressive. No matter what the situation, the chairman must remain placid throughout, and hold the scales fairly between the various parties. Above all, he must be firm and show no weakness. This should not be interpreted to mean, however, that the chairman has the right to brow-beat or bully those who speak. Actually, bullying is a sign of weakness ; it shows that the chairman is uncertain of his own powers and that he adopts extreme measures in order to cloak his deficiencies.

In many ways the chairman of a meeting is like the referee at a football match, and one indispensable qualification is impartiality. It would be hypocritical to say that he must always feel impartial, for if he is an ordinary intelligent human being he will certainly have views, sometimes strong ones, on matters that are argued under his chairmanship. Impartiality means keeping his views to himself. This does not mean only that he must not air them: he must exercise himself to prevent the meeting from inferring what they are. Except on points of procedure the chairman should never seek to express his opinions unless he is specifically asked to do so by the meeting. Nor should he ever try to guide the meeting towards a particular decision, or in any way influence its consideration of the point at issue. In particular he must not show any favouritism towards speakers with whose opinions he is in sympathy, or hostility towards those with whom he personally disagrees.

Normally every speaker must be standing and must address his remarks to the Chair. Only one person at a time is allowed to stand and speak, and one of the Chairman's tasks is to see that this rule is kept. If two or more persons try to speak at the same time he has to decide which should speak first. Sometimes an agreed rotation of speakers will have been decided beforehand, but more commonly, after a motion has been proposed and seconded, the right to speak next goes to whoever is the first to rise. A chairman is not compelled to give any member a hearing, but if he seems to be deliberately excluding anyone, perhaps to favour someone else, he can be overruled by the carrying of a motion " that Mr. — be heard." If such a motion is proposed and seconded, the chairman is bound to put the question to the meeting without further debate, and if it is carried he must enforce it. But this is exceptional, for it can only occur when the chairman is trying to thwart the will of the majority of the meeting.

The chairman must know the rules. He should have a thorough grasp of meeting procedure in general and of the particular rules or by-laws of the body that has met. Like the referee at a football match, again, he should know the rules better than anyone else there. He will lose all respect and therefore authority if, for example, he is caught out on a point of order.

Knowledge of the rules is necessary but should not be flaunted. The best referee is not the one who blows the whistle most frequently, and the chairman must try to keep the meeting going with as few interruptions by himself as he can. He must certainly see that the rules are obeyed, but he should interpret them broadly, according to the spirit rather than in a narrowly legalistic literal sense.

The worst qualification for a chairman is fondness of the sound of one's own voice. Chairmen should be more seen than heard. They should not speak at all unless they have to, and then they should be very brief.

One of the difficulties of chairmanship is the fact that often it is impracticable for everyone to address the meeting for as long as he likes. It may be impossible through lack of time, or undesirable because some speakers are long-winded and stray away from the subject under discussion. Curbing such speakers in the interests of the meeting in general calls for considerable tact. It is not always easy to decide whether the speaker has introduced irrelevant matters —when challenged he usually shows honest surprise— and the chairman should not interfere unless he thinks there is no other way of bringing the speaker back to the matter in hand. The chairman should be very, very reluctant to use his power, after warning the speaker, to order him to stop speaking and sit down. Hurt pride rouses feelings of grievance, and after such action there is usually at least one member of the meeting who has lost confidence in the chairman's impartiality. For this reason it is often a good thing to have a general time-limit on all speeches, which may perhaps be three minutes (the proposer of the motion could be allowed more). The chairman does not have to enforce this to the second, but if speakers need to be curbed this automatic mechanical brake is likely to arouse less resentment than a personal order from the chair.

While the chairman should be in general be tactful, courteous, and benign, never bossy or schoolmasterish, he must also show that when necessary he can be firm. While he should do as little as possible himself to impede the orderly flow of the meeting, he must not tolerate interruptions by anyone else. He can—and should—still be courteous, but he must not be weak or timid in calling to order persons who interrupt a speaker or whisper audibly during a speech. The only permitted interruption is on a point of order, when another member may rise and raise a specific point. The chairman must decide on the point quickly and definitely, without allowing any debate or discussion. Having decided, he must stand by his decision. If he shows any weakness or half-heartedness he will lose respect for the chair.

This respect is vital if order is to be kept. Except when it can be supported by physical threats—as, for example, in schools or prisons or Her Majesty's Forces —discipline depends on voluntary submission to authority, and that is only granted when the authority is regarded with general respect.

Thus it all come to this: A chairman must allow all sides to voice their opinions ; he must be fair to all : he must have no opinions of his own if the harmony of the meeting is likely to be endangered by their expression: he must be genially disposed to all sides: and he must see to it that there is no wavering from the real business in hand.

An Outline of the Chairman's Duties.—So far, we have dealt with the chairman's duties in a general way. Now, we will explain how a meeting should be conducted.

At every meeting the chairman has six definite duties to perform. If he is new to the work, it will be a good idea to write the six items on a slip of paper and have them in front of him while the meeting is proceeding. There will, then, be no fear of missing any vital point.

They are:

(i) *To make sure that the meeting has been convened correctly.*

In most cases there will be no doubt about this. The summons paper states the time, place and other particulars. These will, of course, be adhered to. For instance, it would be unpardonable to start ten minutes early.

Another point to note under this head is that many societies or bodies have a rule in their by-laws which specifies that members must receive notice of a meeting at least a certain period of time in advance. The chairman must satisfy himself that the proper notice has been given. As a matter of fact, he will do this before the meeting.

(ii) *To see that a quorum is present.*

In the by-laws, articles of association, rules, etc., of a body, it is invariably laid down that a certain minimum number of persons is required to be present at a meeting to make the meeting valid. When the minimum number is present, a quorum is formed and the meeting can proceed. It is the chairman's duty to see that this point is observed.

(iii) *To state the purpose of the meeting.*

The chairman opens the meeting by stating its purpose and reading the items on the agenda paper, unless each member has received a copy in which case the chairman merely refers to it and announces that the meeting will proceed to deal with the first item. This is usually the minutes of the last meeting.

(iv) *To have the minutes read of the previous meeting.*

The chairman calls upon the secretary to read them, if there was a previous meeting, and when the reading is finished, he says, " Gentlemen, is it your pleasure that I sign these minutes as correct ?" On an assent being given, the secretary passes the minutes to the chairman, who signs them and adds the date.

The minutes need not be read if a brief printed copy has been sent to members, but the procedure for signing them is the same. Usually approval is indicated by a show of hands, although sometimes the chairman may ask for a proposer and seconder. No motion or discussion of the minutes is allowed before they are confirmed, except in regard to their literal accuracy. After they have been confirmed, however, members of the meeting may ask questions or make comments on any matters arising out of them. This, indeed, is usually the second item on the agenda paper, and in that case the chairman asks the meeting if anyone has any questions or comments.

(v) *To have any correspondence read.*

Usually this is the third item on the agenda. The chairman simply calls upon the secretary to read any correspondence that he has received, touching upon the meeting, or to tell the meeting the contents of the letters. Usually this correspondence consists of letters and telegrams from members expressing regret at their inability to be present.

(vi) *To proceed with as much of the business set down on the agenda as time allows.*

This, of course, is the real work that the meeting has been called to perform. It may begin with the chairman's report, and then perhaps other reports. Then there may be motions and perhaps amendments ; votes of thanks ; and, probably, a final announcement by the chairman of the date and place of the next meeting.

Finally the chairman declares the meeting closed.

DISTURBANCES.—There is no doubt that the Englishman's love of fair play is such that at most meetings the chairman has little difficulty, if he possesses tact, in keeping order. But although he will seldom need to fall back on stern measures, it is highly important that he should know how to act when disorder does occur.

The Public Meeting Act, 1908, provides that any person at a lawful public meeting who acts in a disorderly manner for the purpose of preventing the transaction of the business for which the meeting was called is guilty of an offence, and on conviction is liable to a fine not exceeding £5 or imprisonment not exceeding one month. The Public Order Act, 1936, provides that any person at a public meeting who uses threatening, abusive, or insulting words or behaviour with intent to provoke a breach of the peace, or whereby a breach of the peace is likely to be caused, is guilty of an offence, and on conviction is liable to imprisonment not exceeding three months or to a fine not exceeding £50 or to both imprisonment and fine. A constable without warrant may arrest any person whom he reasonably suspects of committing an offence under the 1936 Act. Further, he may, if asked by the chairman of the meeting, require such a person to declare to him immediately his name and address, and if the person refuses he is guilty of an offence and is liable on conviction to a fine not exceeding forty shillings.

It is rare, however, that the law will need to be invoked. Usually, the utmost which a chairman will feel disposed to do is to declare the meeting closed and, when he has left the chair, all further discussion is without value. Or he can adjourn the meeting for a definite period of time. This is usually the better plan, as to close the meeting sacrifices the whole of the occasion. An adjournment for, say, fifteen minutes loses no more time than is needed to enable the disorderly element to come to its senses.

A POINT OF ORDER.—It is very clear that occasions may arise when the person who is speaking permits himself to make some offensive remark. The remark may consist of insulting or improper language, or one of a thousand other things. Generally, the chairman will immediately interfere ; but it is clear that the remark may be of such a character that the chairman is not to know of its derogatory nature. When this occurs, it is open to anyone in the hall to rise and interrupt the speaker. He uses the formula, " Mr. Chairman, I rise on a point of order." He does not wait for the speaker to finish his speech and he need not wait for a pause in his words ; he simply talks louder than the one who has made the offensive remark. The original speaker must give way to allow the interrupter to say what the point of order is, and the chairman then has to decide whether or not the interrupter was correct in drawing his attention to it. If a remark is considered offensive the speaker is normally required to withdraw it.

If a member notices an irregularity or error in procedure that has escaped the attention of the chairman —for example, if there is not a quorum or if the wording of a motion is faulty—he may similarly interrupt on a point of order. Similar action may be taken by any member if, for example, whispering is going on and the chairman is not using his authority to stop it.

CHAPTER III

THE DUTIES OF THE SECRETARY

THE secretary is a very important official, whether we are thinking of a company, a society or any other body of people. Though he ranks below the chairman, it often happens that his knowledge of relevant matters is greater than that of his chief ; in fact, the chairman frequently turns to him for the facts which he requires.

These remarks apply to all secretaries, but in other respects there are very important differences between a company secretary and all other secretaries, honorary or paid. The company secretary has certain duties that are legally defined in the Companies Act, 1948, and if he fails in these duties — even through obeying the orders of the board—he is liable to heavy penalties.

The company secretary's duties are mainly executive and clerical. He does not normally initiate or direct—unlike, for example. the honorary secretary of a social or sports club, who is often the driving force.

NOTICE FOR MEETINGS.—Most bodies other than companies give notice of meetings either at previous meetings or by displaying a notice in some prominent place. Sometimes, however, the rules or standing orders lay down that an individual notice must be sent to every person who is entitled to receive it and to attend the meeting. In the case of companies it is laid down by law that this procedure should be followed. In all cases giving notice of meetings is the responsibility of the secretary.

A statutory notice of a meeting must include not only the date and place but also full information about the purpose or purposes for which the meeting is to be held. Important items of business should not be concealed under the vague heading " Any Other Business," which is included for minor and incidental affairs. Information must also be included about the appointment of proxies who are entitled to attend and vote in place of members.

Under the Companies Act, 1948, every company must hold a general meeting at least once every calendar year and not more than fifteen months after the preceding general meeting (except in the case of the first annual general meeting, which must be held within eighteen months of the company's incorporation). This annual general meeting and any meeting called for the passing of a special resolution must be called by at least twenty-one days' notice in writing ; for other meetings fourteen days' notice is required, and for unlimited companies the minimum period is seven days. These are statutory requirements and must be fulfilled irrespective of the rules or standing orders of the company. Periods of notice are reckoned as clear days—that is, the number excludes the day of sending the notice and the day of the meeting.

THE AGENDA.—The notices of the meeting having been posted, the secretary must now busy himself with the agenda. This is a brief résumé of the business that is to be transacted. Sometimes a copy of the agenda is sent out with the notice of the meeting. Here is a specimen, with the notes, added in brackets, which the secretary would be likely to write on it, as soon as the matters were decided at the actual meeting:

AGENDA

(1) Minutes of the last meeting.
    (Signed by the chairman.)

(2) Matters arising from the minutes.

(3) Correspondence.

(4) Reports.

(5) Finance.
    (Pass book put in showing a favourable bank balance of £853 10s. 2d.)

(6) Purchase of a sports ground at New Leighton.
    (To purchase the ground at the agreed price of £500.)

(7) To discuss the advisability or otherwise of holding literary meetings twice monthly during the winter session.)
    (Rejected by 27 votes to 22.)

(8) Fixing a date for the next meeting.
    (November 13th, 19—.)

THE MEETING.—When the meeting is about to begin, the secretary will see that all the arrangements for the reception and comfort of the members have been carried out. Then he will take his seat on the platform, usually at the chairman's elbow. He is needed here because it is to him that the chairman turns when he wishes to know a fact, such as a set of figures, or needs the production of a document.

The secretary, if he is a thorough and capable official, listens intently throughout the proceedings and does his best to anticipate things. Thus, when the chairman is speaking and he happens to mention a document, the secretary has already run through his papers and, just when the document is referred to, he hands it to the chairman, who is able to consult it without the loss of a second.

It is evident from this that the secretary, more than anybody, must keep his mind on the course of events, for not only is he the chairman's mainstay, but he has much to do in the way of making notes recording the decisions and conduct of the meeting. These notes he needs for such purposes as the next set of minutes.

It often happens that a dozen trivial things will arise while the meeting is in progress. As the secretary acts in the capacity of a manager, these trivial things will be set before him and they will distract him from the serious work of the meeting. Accordingly, the wise secretary will appoint a " junior " who will act on his own initiative when trumpery matters have to be dealt with.

Of course, the secretary is called upon to read the notice of the meeting and the minutes when the meeting opens. This is the only time he has to speak, unless the chairman calls upon him to read a document or explain something that has arisen out of his duties. Usually, a secretary's speech is no more than a brief recital of facts, and always, it is as short as the matter permits.

After the meeting the secretary will see that all documents are safely collected and carried away, that servants are paid, and it often happens that he has to pacify a member who harbours a grievance. Nominally, he is the last to leave the hall.

CHAPTER IV

THE MINUTES OF A MEETING

It would be useless for a number of people to come together and deliberate on matters of importance to them were no record kept of their actions and findings. Accordingly a history of every meeting of any importance is always compiled. The author of the history is the secretary, and what he writes down is known as the " minutes."

So that the minutes can be preserved and easily consulted, at any future time, every society, company, body or other gathering which meets regularly, possesses a minute book in which these records are placed one after the other, in chronological order.

As will be appreciated, the minutes must be very carefully written in order that they record faithfully exactly what happens at each meeting. In extreme cases, the minutes may be used as evidence in courts of law ; thus their accuracy must be above suspicion.

Drawing up The Minutes of a Meeting.—Every secretary will not reproduce the minutes of a meeting in exactly the same way ; indeed, much latitude in their arrangement is allowed. Still, a certain amount of uniformity is advisable, and it is best to plan them on the following lines:

(i) Date, hour and place where the meeting was held.

(ii) Name of the chairman.

(iii) Names of other officials who were present, and total number of members who attended. In small gatherings, the names of everybody present may be mentioned.

(iv) An account of the formalities gone through, before the actual business was reached. This includes such matters as the secretary's reading of the notice convening the meeting, and the reading of the previous meeting.

(v) An outline of the actual business transacted.

(vi) Date fixed for the next meeting, if this was agreed upon.

(vii) Time when the meeting closed.

All the above headings are perfectly straightforward with the exception of (v), which needs some explanation. In this section, all motions must be given in the exact form in which they were put from the chair. So that this may be done, it is usual to require the proposer to write down the wording of his motion. Then the secretary can copy the exact words into the minutes.

With each motion should be given the name of the proposer and the seconder ; also the state of the voting. In addition, mention should be made of any question which was withdrawn, negatived or superseded.

A SPECIMEN SET OF MINUTES.—In order that the above hints may be still more useful to secretaries unfamiliar with their work, the following specimen set of minutes has been drawn up.

Minutes of the Tenth Ordinary Meeting of the Riverside Debating Society, held on January 12th, 19—, in the Empress Rooms, at 7.30 p.m.

The chair was taken by Mr. A.

The following members were present: Messrs. B. C. D. etc. ; also Mrs. L. M. N. etc., and Miss O.

The secretary, Mr. P., was also present.

The notice calling the meeting was read by the secretary, who followed by reading the minutes of the Ninth Ordinary Meeting, held on October 5th, 19—. These minutes were confirmed by those present and signed by the chairman.

Letters of apology were read from Messrs. Q. and R., who regretted their inability to be present, the former on account of illness and the latter from business pressure.

A letter was read from the Secretary of the local hospital accepting the society's offer to give a concert to the patients some time during the month of February.

Upon the motion of Mr. B. and seconded by Mr. C., it was resolved, unanimously, that the programme and other details of the presentation be entrusted to Mr. D., Miss O. and the secretary.

A long discussion then ensued regarding the growing funds of the society in the bank, and it was moved by Mr. C., and seconded by Miss O., that £20 be expended on refurnishing the Club room.

An amendment was moved by Mr. D., and seconded by Mrs. L., that the sum be increased to £50 ; but this was rejected by the meeting. (Votes 10 for, 15 against.)

The original motion was then put to the meeting and carried by a majority of 20 votes.

Mrs. M. then made the complaint that the Library was in a neglected condition, that certain books had been borrowed and never returned ; whilst others had suffered defacement that was not ordinary wear and tear. She proposed, and Mrs. N. seconded, a motion to the effect that a committee of four be appointed to enquire into a more up-to-date system of classifying, lending and preserving the books.

The motion was put to the meeting and carried unanimously.

Upon a motion proposed by Miss O., and seconded by Mr. B., it was unanimously agreed that the committee consist of Mrs. M., Mrs. N., Mr. C., and the secretary.

As there was no further business, the meeting terminated at 10.15 p.m., after a vote of thanks was accorded to the chairman.

DOCUMENTS AND THE MINUTE BOOK.—Since the minute book is a record or history of a body or society's activities, it follows that no better place for preserving certain documents could be found than in the minute book. Thus, in most minute books one finds inserted such things as agendas, letters, receipts, contracts, etc.

CHAPTER V

MOTIONS AND AMENDMENTS

MOTIONS are usually put before meetings in one of two ways. The most suitable method is for a member to send the actual wording of his proposal to the secretary at least a specified number of days before the matter is to come up at a meeting. In the by-laws of many societies, a definite time is mentioned by these notices.

On receiving the motion, the secretary considers it and, if it is in order, he places it on the agenda of the next meeting. He is bound to deal with it in this way if it is relevant and received within the prescribed period of time. He cannot shelve it, for instance, until another occasion, on the grounds that the business of the meeting is already too heavy. The only way in which the motion may be deprived of a hearing is for the chairman to close or adjourn the meeting before the particular item has been reached on the agenda.

Though a motion should always be sent to the secretary in advance of the meeting, whenever such a course is practicable, it is evident that circumstances must arise which often make it impossible. We will suppose, for instance, that while the meeting is in progress and some matter is being discussed, a member offers his opinions on a certain point. These opinions are, perhaps, of more than ordinary moment. As a result, the chairman may say, " Mr. X., will you put that in the form of a motion ? " and then, Mr. X. frames a motion. Clearly, such a motion could not be sent to the secretary seven days in advance of the meeting.

From what has been said, it may be inferred that, when clear matters of policy are concerned, notice should be given of the motion ; but no notice is needed, or even possible, when the matter concerns such things as the appointment of a temporary chairman, the adjournment of a meeting, the formation of a committee to undertake special work, the business connected with letters read at the meeting, and issues arising out of the speeches of the members.

Many bodies require all motions dealing with questions of policy to be:

(i) Set out in writing.

(ii) Received by the secretary, a given number of days before the meeting. Seven, ten or twenty-one days are usually specified.

(iii) Entered in a special book by the secretary. Such motions are to be brought before the meeting in the order in which they figure in the book.

(iv) Proposed by the members who furnished them.

But, as we have already indicated, whether a motion is framed before or during a meeting, the proposer should set it down in writing, so that no mistake may be made about its actual wording. In addition, it should always take an affirmative form, beginning with the word " That." Thus, the correct commencement is " That this or that is to be . . . ", " That X should be done. . . . "

DEALING WITH MOTIONS.—A motion is set before a meeting by its proposer. This person stands and explains what he has in view, either commencing or ending his remarks by repeating the actual words of the motion.

When he has finished, he sits and, then, it is open to anyone to second it. Legally a seconder is unnecessary, but most standing orders and rules of societies require that every motion should have a seconder as well as a proposer. In this case, suppose nobody is willing to act as seconder. The chairman will wait a suitable period of time and then declare that the motion has failed, as it lacks a seconder. The issue is now closed and cannot be reopened during the course of the same meeting.

But it is more likely that someone will second the proposer's motion. The motion being proposed and seconded, it is now open for debate. Anyone in the room may speak on the subject, but not more than once. The exception to this rule is the proposer. It is only fair that he, who began the discussion, should have an opportunity of closing it. Thus, he alone may speak twice on the same motion.

AMENDMENTS.—It is very obvious that when a motion is before a meeting there will be people present who, while sympathising with the motion, may feel that it, perhaps, goes too far or not far enough; or they may think that by an alteration of the wording the effect will be clearer, stronger, or, in some way, more what is wanted. Accordingly, they wish to make alterations in the motion, and this they do by proposing what is known as an amendment to the original motion.

Of course, it sometimes happens that a person who wants to defeat a motion, rises and suggests that the word " not " be inserted in some suitable place. This word, therefore, has the effect of changing the whole aim of the motion and making it the exact opposite to what was originally intended. Needless to say, this is an unfair amendment, and any live chairman will quickly rule it out of order. He should point out to the proposer of the amendment that his proper course is to speak against the original motion and hope that the voting will reject it.

THREE FORMS OF AMENDMENTS.—Amendments may take one of three forms:

(i) Words may be omitted from the original motion.

(ii) Words may be added to the original motion.

(iii) Words in the original motion may be changed.

To explain the working of these different kinds of amendments, we have selected the following motion and will submit it to the three processes:

" That this meeting deplores the use of juvenile labour in the local depot, seeing that the premises are not of an approved nature."

Case 1.—The chairman rises and reads the original motion and then adds that he has received an amendment which proposes to leave out the words "juvenile labour in." "The question I have to propose," he adds, " is that the words named do form part of the motion." If the votes favour their inclusion, then the chairman asks if there are any other amendments and, failing others, he puts the original motion to the vote. But, if the votes favour their exclusion and there are no other amendments, the original motion, duly altered, is voted on in this form, " That this meeting deplores the use of the local depot, seeing that the premises are not of an approved nature."

Case 2.—The chairman rises and reads out the original motion and then adds that he has received an amendment which proposes to add the words " adult and," following the words " That this meeting deplores the use of." " The question I have to propose," he adds, " is that the words named do form part of the motion and be inserted where suggested." If the votes favour the amendment and no other amendments are offered, he puts the original motion, duly altered, to the vote. It then runs as follows: " That this meeting deplores the use of adult and juvenile labour in the local depot, seeing that the premises are not of an approved nature." But if the votes do not favour the amendment, and no other amendments are forthcoming, the original motion is put to the vote.

Case 3.—The third case may present great difficulties. The chairman rises and reads the original motion and then adds that he has received an amendment which proposes to substitute the words " adult labour can be found in plenty," instead of " the premises are not of an approved nature." " The question I have to propose," he adds, " is that the original words named do form part of the motion." If the votes favour their inclusion, the amendment fails and the motion as it stood at first is put to the meeting. If, however, the votes favour their exclusion, the chairman then puts the question as to whether the new words shall be added. The previous voting presumed that the new words are to be included but, in debates, nothing is certain, and the voting may go against the inclusion of the new words. What, then, is the chairman to do?

It is quite conceivable that a motion with words omitted might be meaningless, although in the above case some meaning is still attached to the abbreviated sentence. The chairman should ask that alternative words be suggested but, failing any, he must put the original motion, minus the words in question, to the vote.

AMENDMENTS TO AMENDMENTS.—While on the subject, it will be well to point out that an amendment can be proposed to an amendment. In fact, such are not at all rare at meetings where the debate becomes tense.

When an amendment is suggested to a previous amendment, the position becomes somewhat involved unless the issues are kept clearly in mind. The best plan is to dismiss the original motion from mind for the time being, and to look upon the first amendment as a motion, and the second amendment as a simple amendment to the newly-created motion. The second amendment is, then, discussed and, if it succeeds upon a vote, the original amendment is altered accordingly. This newly-worded amendment is, next, put up for discussion, and if it is voted upon favourably, the original motion is turned to once more but with the amending words. The rule, therefore, with amendments and motions is to work backwards and to deal with the smallest issues first, the greatest issues last.

HOW AMENDMENTS ARE REGULATED.—It will have been recognised already that amendments are treated in much the same way as motions. They are, in fact, small portions of motions. Thus, whenever possible, notice of an amendment should be given in advance, exactly as has been described for motions ; but it is quite clear that the opportunities for giving notice will be fewer than in the case of motions.

Continuing, an amendment must be put forward by a proposer, and this person may be allowed to speak twice, although this is not an automatic right as in the case of the proposer of a motion. By custom, the amendment must, like the motion, find a seconder but again by law it need not. As in the case of a motion, there is usually a local rule which specifically states that an amendment may not be voted upon unless it has been seconded. Then the chairman drops any amendment that is unseconded.

Before leaving the question, it is necessary to emphasise what has already been said, that the practice in most debates is to take the vote on an amendment before the vote on its motion. This, however, is not universal, since the opposite course is observed in the Houses of Parliament. Therefore, in all political debating societies, the Parliamentary plan will be preferred ; elsewhere the amendment will come before the motion.

CHAPTER VI

CLOSURES AND ADJOURNMENTS

EVERYBODY who has to attend meetings frequently, knows that much valuable time is wasted through the verbosity of certain speakers. How often, for instance, have we all been forced to listen for half an hour to a speech which could have been made in five minutes? The answer, probably, is "many times." As a rule, these lengthy orations are delivered by speakers who love to hear their own voices, but there are occasions when speeches are made to drag on and on purposely to waste time and to prevent discussion on other matters.

More often than not, a little judicious fidgeting on the part of the listeners has its intended effect on a wordy debater, and he promptly sits down. But the man who purposely speaks on and on, in order to waste time, is not deterred by such trifles. He is too thick skinned for that.

Thus it comes about that a method of stopping a speaker has had to be evolved, and the rules which govern the method are known as the closure rules.

It is very evident that any set of rules having for their object the muzzling of the speakers must be carefully handled, or the rules may do more harm than good. Suppose, for instance, that someone in the hall wishes to silence a speaker because the latter is divulging facts that are unpleasant to him and his friends. What he will do will be to invoke the closure system, and, unless the majority of the members are too alert for him, he will gain his ends. All this shows very clearly that while the closure rules are a valuable weapon, they must only be applied judiciously.

CLOSURE RULES AND HOW THEY ARE APPLIED.—It is close on midnight, we will suppose, and somebody has been making a rambling speech for the last three-quarters of an hour. Members are casting anxious glances at the clock, and somebody murmurs, " Will he never sit down? " This is a suitable occasion for invoking the closure system. A member rises and proposes " That the question be now put."

(a) This member can usually only succeed with his proposal if the total time of all the speakers on the particular debate has lasted, at least, one hour. The time taken by the present speaker does not, alone, count.

(b) Whenever possible, the proposer should aim rather at preventing other speakers from following on than bringing a present speaker to a stop. This however, is a matter of courtesy ; and he can stand at any moment and make his proposal, even during the middle of a sentence.

(c) The speaker must, then, stop immediately and await the decision of the meeting.

(d) The chairman must follow the rules of his society, association, etc. In some cases, the rules give him the choice of action. He may over-ride the proposal, if he thinks it unreasonable ; or he may proceed with it. In other cases, he is bound to consider the proposal of closing. It depends on the rules of the particular body.

(*e*) When an amendment is under discussion, the closure motion only applies to the amendment. Further debate is still possible on the original motion.

(*f*) If the chairman agrees to the proposal, the member moving it shall be allowed to speak for not more than five minutes. After the motion has been seconded, without a speech, and one member has been heard in opposition, for not more than five minutes, the question shall be put at once without further debate.

(*g*) If the voting favours the motion " That the question be now put," it is the usual practice to allow the member who proposed the motion or amendment which has been under discussion for so long a time to close the debate upon it. Whether he has any right in this matter or not is doubtful, and it is more than probable that custom merely allows him this privilege out of courtesy. Therefore, it is incumbent on him to say what he wants as briefly as possible.

(*h*) When the closure motion fails and the discussion goes on, it is quite conceivable that, after a lapse of some time, a second closure motion may be suggested. There is nothing, in fact, to prevent half a dozen such motions, if the members happen to be in the temper to propose them. There is only one rule about them, which is that nobody may propose or second a closure motion more than once at the same meeting.

What we have been discussing above is called the ordinary closure. A discussion on a motion may also be limited by a form of closure called a guillotine. The purpose of this is to speed up the business of a meeting by setting a time-limit to discussion: then, when the time is up, whether the discussion is closed or not, the chairman is bound to close it and put the motion to the vote. For a guillotine closure the form of motion is "that discussion on such-and-such a motion be limited to so many hours and minutes."

A third form of closure is what is called the kangaroo. This is only adopted when there are a number of amendments that seem likely to prolong the discussion beyond a reasonable time. This is avoided by allowing the chairman to jump from one amendment to another, leaving out those in between. Naturally he picks the amendments that he thinks most important. Often it is his suggestion that this method should be adopted and the meeting accepts this without a formal motion. If a formal motion is needed, however, it is simply "that the chairman be allowed to make a selection of the amendments."

THE PREVIOUS QUESTION.—When a motion (but not an amendment to it) is under discussion, any member of the meeting who has not spoken on the motion may move the "Previous Question." The purpose of this is to prevent a decision on the motion from being taken. Often the "Previous Question" is not moved until the debate on the motion has been in progress for some time—indeed, it may be deliberately delayed in order that opinions on the subject should be freely expressed: for it is the vote, not the free discussion, that is under fire.

So the " Previous Question " is normally moved at the end of a speech. When it has been proposed—and seconded, if the rules of the organization make this necessary—there may be discussion although this is not always desirable. The form of motion may be either " I move the Previous Question " or simply " that the question be not now put." No amendment can be made to the original motion after the motion for a " Previous Question " has been made. If the motion for the " Previous Question " is carried, the original motion is wiped out. If it is not carried, the original motion is immediately put to the vote without further discussion.

THE NEXT BUSINESS.—A motion " that this meeting do proceed to the next business " may be made at the close of any speech during a discussion, whether of the original motion or an amendment, and if it is seconded and carried it has the same effect as the " Previous Question." If the motion is not carried, the discussion continues: and usually there is a definite limit of time before this motion can be moved again on the same subject of discussion.

ADJOURNMENT OF A DEBATE.—A debate may be adjourned to give the members of the meeting an opportunity to obtain more information on the subject or to give the matter further thought before a decision is taken. The motion to adjourn the debate should not be moved until the conclusion of a speech. It should be in the form " that this discussion be adjourned to ——", with the time or date. The adjournment of the debate does not interfere with the continuation of the meeting for the transaction of other business. The person who moves the motion for the adjournment of a debate normally has the right to reopen the discussion when it is resumed, whether this is later in the same meeting or at a meeting at a later date.

ADJOURNMENT OF A MEETING.—The motion to adjourn the meeting may be made at the conclusion of any speech. It may thus serve to prevent a vote being taken on the motion under discussion at the time. Usually it is put forward to close a meeting that has gone on too long or ceased to function usefully perhaps because tempers are frayed.

The motion should be in the form "that the business of this meeting be adjourned to the next ordinary meeting "—or to a particular date and time, if the motion is to resume the interrupted discussion at a special meeting. This is a point that must be made quite clear by the wording of the motion. Unless a date and time are fixed it may be generally assumed that the adjournment will be until the next ordinary meeting, but members should be told the position before they vote.

If a motion to adjourn a meeting is defeated, it may be proposed again after a reasonable lapse of time.

CHAPTER VII

VOTING AT MEETINGS

A CHAIRMAN, who is not well versed in his duties, may be a little perplexed when it comes to taking a vote of the members present. In order that he may have the matter at his finger tips, we propose to set out all the necessary rules on the subject in this chapter. It will entail a slight amount of repetition of information given in other chapters, but the question is of importance and well worth the space devoted to it.

THE SPOKEN VOTE.—As a rule, the usual way of expressing one's preference is to raise a hand at the proper moment, but in many assemblies the vote is spoken. This statement, of course, needs explaining.

Therefore, we will suppose that the chairman has reached the stage when he puts the question. He rises and says, " The question is that this assembly is firmly of the opinion . . . " and so on. He pauses a second and then says something to this effect, "As many as are of this opinion, say Aye." There are shouts in the affirmative coming from the members. When they have died down, he continues with, "As many as are of the contrary opinion, say No." There are more shouts, but this time they are of a negative order. The chairman assesses the two and say, " I think the Ayes (or the

Noes) have it," whichever is the case. Then, he waits a second, because let it be marked, he has not said definitely that one side or the other has won, merely that he thinks so.

If nothing happens and nobody challenges him, the voting is finished, as far as that motion is concerned. But he may be challenged.

VOTING BY A SHOW OF HANDS.—When members disagree with his opinion of the spoken vote, the chairman must proceed to take a vote by a show of hands. More often than not, the spoken vote is omitted from the proceedings and voting by hand is done at once.

When a vote is to be taken by hands, the chairman, usually, appoints a teller for and against, and these two gentlemen do the counting in turn. Naturally, others check the numbers, and what the tellers report to the chairman may be taken as correct. The chairman then stands and reads out the numbers, declaring the result of the voting accordingly.

CARD AND PROXY VOTING.—In large organizations voting is sometimes by card, and this is commonly called card or block voting. A representative of each society or branch entitled to vote carries a card with the appropriate number of votes inscribed on it in large figures. When a question is put, the representative holds up the card so that the teller may add the number to the total votes cast for or against the motion, as the case may be.

A proxy is a written permission, signed by the person giving the permission, permitting someone else to vote for him. Proxy voting is especially common at meetings of the shareholders of a company, who may number several thousands and are unlikely all to want to attend.

DEMAND FOR A POLL.—It is laid down in the Companies Act that at a meeting of shareholders, on a show of hands every member present in person (or his proxy) shall have one vote, and that on a poll every member (or his proxy) shall have one vote for each share of which he is the holder.

Therefore unless a poll is demanded, the chairman at a shareholders' meeting has only to count the hands put up for and against each motion and declare the result. A simple majority is usually sufficient unless a specified larger majority is stipulated.

A demand for a poll must be made by a specified minimum number of shareholders or by a shareholder or shareholders representing a specified minimum proportion of the total voting rights. The person or persons demanding the poll must state their names and holdings of shares and the motion on which the poll is demanded. The secretary must verify these qualifications from the share register, and then the chairman will make the necessary announcement to the meeting and decide when and where the poll will take place. It may be taken immediately or at some future date.

CHAPTER VIII

COMMITTEES AND THEIR FORMATION

FREQUENTLY, a society or other body is faced with a matter that needs very careful consideration. In the ordinary way, the matter is one that the full body of members could not profitably discuss. It may be that they have not the requisite knowledge to deal with technical points, or perhaps they lack the time needed for sifting all the relevant evidence.

When such a matter arises, it is usual for a committee to be formed to go into the questions and report to the full body of members. The committee is comparatively small in numbers and it is a well known fact that a small group of people can often settle down to a task and accomplish it, while a large number of such people would never make any headway at all.

The committee, though it is sanctioned by the full body or society, has no power to bind the society. It merely deliberates, sifts all the available evidence, and then reports to the society. The latter receives the report and acts upon it or not, according to its own wishes. As is well known, Parliament has set up thousands of such committees, and it may be added, ninety per cent. of the reports have been set aside and never acted upon.

When a committee is to be formed for some specific purpose, the first consideration is its size. Naturally, if a body of a dozen men is appointing a committee, the committee will be considerably smaller than if a body of a hundred men are creating it. But, in every case, the great thing is to keep the number down to its smallest limits, consistent with usefulness. Five is, perhaps, as low as one may reasonably go, while twenty is approaching the maximum.

In creating a committee, the full body of members will be wise if they fetter the committee with as few restrictions as possible. The matter to be deliberated on should be very definitely set out and then perhaps a date for receiving the report should be named. The committee is then free to appoint its own chairman, make its own rules and set about the task before it exactly as it thinks fit.

Clearly, the first thing a committee must do is to appoint its chairman and then decide on what is to form a quorum. The lowest number for a quorum should be three—two is quite unsatisfactory—while five is an average number for a fairly large committee.

Procedure at the meetings which are held is quite formal. Members often sit round a table and discuss business as though they were chatting on friendly matters. Nobody stands when speaking, and the rules about speaking once to a motion and similar things are waived entirely. Even a motion need not be seconded.

After all the points for consideration have been dealt with *in extenso* and all the witnesses examined, the committee draws up its report. On occasions when a committee has not been able to arrive at a unanimous conclusion, a minority report as well as a majority report is submitted to the full body, but this plan is contrary to the strict rules, and, if it is at all possible, one report only should be drawn up.

As a rule, when the committee has completed the first draft of the report, it appoints a day and then considers the report paragraph by paragraph, each section being treated as a motion which is capable of amendment. When the full draft has been dealt with in this manner, a vote is taken to the effect " that this report be submitted to the full society or other body."

When the full society receives the report it is considered and acted upon or not, according to the opinions of the majority. On occasion, the information furnished by the committee is used in a modified form. Not more than fifty per cent. of the reports, so drawn up, are accepted by the central body in their entirety. This should not be taken as a slight on the members of the committee. Their point of view generally differs very considerably from that of the central body, which has to deal not only with questions of fact but also of policy.

The committee described above is what is generally called a special or *ad hoc* committee: that is to say, it is appointed for a particular purpose, and when this has been achieved it is wound up or dissolved.

There are a number of other kinds of committees, most of which follow much the same procedure.

First of all, there is the executive committee, which

is elected at the annual general meeting and is normally responsible for the actual management of the organization.

Then there is the standing committee, a permanent committee set up annually to carry out administrative work of some particular kind.

Finally there is the joint committee, which is set up by two or more bodies and usually has to try to co-ordinate their activities in some way. It may be a permanent or special committee.

A sub-committee is, as the name implies, an off-shoot of a committee of one kind or another, created to relieve the larger body of some of the detailed work.

Decisions of committees—that is, motions that are carried—are recorded in the form of recommendations. Decisions of general meetings, on the other hand, go down as resolutions.

CHAPTER IX

THE CHAIRMAN AT A DINNER

MANY a good dinner has been spoilt for someone because the person in question has been called upon to take the chair. After all, the duties of a chairman on these occasions are pleasant enough and, once the formalities are understood, the rest should be easy.

PREPARING THE TOAST LIST.—We will suppose that you have been singled out for the post of chairman at a forthcoming dinner, your first care will then be to give an eye to the toast list. Usually, there is some official who has done this work before and to whom you may safely leave such matters. Still, you are nominally responsible and your best plan is to get into touch with the official and talk over the plans. In any case, whether you actually draw up the list or not, it is advisable that you should know, in advance, exactly what the arrangements are.

THE DINNER.—When the guests have assembled at their tables, it is the usual custom for the toastmaster to " knock up " and say in a loud voice, " Pray be silent while your chairman says grace." With everybody standing, you then repeat grace, that is if your society has no official chaplain, or there is no clergyman present who will accept the duty. Then the dinner begins, and for some little time, you are free to enjoy the courses without any interruption. However, after a while, the moment arrives for the first toast, which is invariably " The Queen."

To give this toast, your toastmaster or you will knock to gain attention and then you will stand and say, " Ladies and Gentlemen (or whatever is applicable), The Queen." Everyone stands, holds up his glass and says " The Queen " ; then taking a sip, repeats the words, " The Queen."

THE PERSONAL TOASTS.—Having dealt with what are known as the loyal toasts, a short space of time is allowed to elapse and then you reach what might be called the personal toasts. They are the toasts which intimately affect your assembly, society, etc. Whether one of these will or will not fall to your lot depends on circumstances. If you have ample speakers, then the duties of proposing and replying can be safely left to others ; but when few people are willing to come forward, it is very evident that you will have to propose one of them.

The last of the personal toasts is usually " The Chairman." This will be proposed by a friend of yours and, a few seconds after he has concluded, you will rise and respond. Thus, your duties consist mainly in calling upon the various speakers to propose or reply to the toasts, also in proposing one toast and replying to another. Let it be said that your right-hand man, and not you, calls upon the speaker who is to propose your health.

The final toasts are usually those of " The Visitors," and, or " The Ladies." If the duty devolves on you and not the toastmaster of calling upon the speakers throughout the evening, you will rise and use some such formula as this, " Ladies and Gentlemen, I have great pleasure in calling upon Mr. So and So to propose (or reply to) the toast of *whatever it is*," and then you sit.

When the last speech has been made, the last item on the programme has been given and the proceedings have come to their termination, you must rise and say something by way of a conclusion. Here you have unlimited choice. " Well, Ladies and Gentlemen," you may care to say, " it has been a very successful and enjoyable evening and I am sure you all regret it has come to an end so quickly." With that, you have finished.

CHAPTER X

MANY people will do anything rather than speak in public, whilst others would hardly consider that an occasion had gone off satisfactorily if they had not had an opportunity of hearing their own voices. Of the two, we much prefer the attitude of the former class though, of course, the best plan to adopt is something midway between the two.

Living as we do in a highly organized state, it is a condition forced on us that occasions will occur when we are bound to express our views publicly. We should not try to avoid the occasions, but accept them in their proper light and go ahead. After all is said and done, there is nothing much in it, although our timidity makes us think there is.

Let us suppose that you hold a position—it may be as a director of a company, an official in a golf club, or any post of a public or semi-public nature—and you see looming ahead in the distance the time when you will have to make a full-length speech. Maybe you view the occasion with a shudder and wonder whatever you will do when the moment arrives. Do not think there is any novelty in your position. Thousands before you have felt exactly as you do and, when the occasion has passed, they have wondered why they looked upon it all with such trepidation.

How to Gain Confidence in Public.—Of course, if you are wise, you will say to yourself, " I'm a bad speaker, but I'll put all that right before the big occasion arrives." Now, this is how you will set about putting things right. First, you will go to all the meetings you can and you will take your part in the proceedings. You will get up, for instance, and say " Mr. Chairman, I have great pleasure in seconding that motion," and then you will sit down. These few words are the thin edge of the wedge. You have heard your own voice in public and you have made a start. From this, you will go on to higher flights. An occasion will arise when you will speak for, perhaps, two minutes on a motion, whereas, formerly, you always sat still when discussions were going on. Thus, from small beginnings, you will proceed to bigger things, and become accustomed to hearing your own voice.

Naturally, you are not eager to tell others of your little failings, but it will be just as well to enlist the sympathies of a close friend and ask him to listen intently to anything you may say at the meeting. And, when it is all over, you will get him to tell you whether you pitched your voice loud enough to fill the hall, whether you spoke too softly, or what he thought of it. From his criticisms, you ought to be able to learn just those little things that you could never find out for yourself.

So much for the way you will get accustomed to facing an audience, but you must attend, also, to the technique of your oratory, and this you will do at home. Take yourself into an upper room of your house, close the windows and doors, and then begin by reading aloud some good prose. Stand in front of a mirror, hold the book in your left hand and leave the right hand free to move about. You should put in some actions with your hands, when making a speech, but a great deal is not wanted and it is very easy to overdo this part of the business.

After the prose, turn to one of the specimen speeches in this book and, while reading it, try to imagine that you are actually delivering the speech. Probably, you will be surprised at the progress you will make after three or four practices. And, when you have delivered a few of the specimen speeches, make up some of your own. Choose any subject you fancy and talk aloud on the matter for three of four minutes. That, too, will be excellent practice.

PRONUNCIATION AND VOCABULARY.—Now that you have embarked on speeches of your own, it will be necessary to give a good deal of thought to your pronunciation and vocabulary. In ordinary conversation, many of us use a style that is more or less slovenly, and were someone to write down exactly what we say and how we say it, there is little doubt that we should be amazed, when it was reproduced for our benefit.

Now, in speeches, there are listeners who are noting every syllable and every word we utter. Thus, it is highly important for us to speak well and choose suitable words,—far more so than it is in ordinary conversation.

The use of the aspirate and the pronunciation of some of the more unfamiliar of our words should be given the first consideration. It is quite common to hear such expressions as " izzee " for " is he," and " he-oo " for " he who." These are the very natural results of rapid and slurred speech, and will disappear if a speaker will but remember to deliver each word separately and deliberately. A far more irritating defect, and one much more difficult to eradicate, is the habit of misplacing the aspirate. In their desire not to admit it, some people tack the letter " h " on to almost every word beginning with a vowel. Misuse of the letter " h " is frequently the result of a failure to observe a very useful rule regarding the pronunciation of the common word " the." Before a vowel, the word " the " should be pronounced as " thee " ; before an " h," it should be pronounced as the letters " th " in the word " leather." Many people invert this rule, and the result is such errors as " the hambition " and " the 'ouse."

Another common defect is the addition of an " r " at the end of a word which ends with a vowel, such as " the idear of."

A speaker should aim continually at the extension of his vocabulary. Nevertheless, in speech, the familiar word should always be given preference over the far-fetched, the short over the long, and the concise phrase over circumlocution.

One still finds many people with extremely hazy ideas regarding the difference in meaning and pronunciation between such words as complaisant and complacent, deprecate and depreciate, ascetic and aesthetic, veracity and voracity, allusion and illusion, proscribe and prescribe, perspicacity and perspicuity. These and doubtless many others will repay looking up in a good dictionary.

Then, again, certain verbs are often wrongly used. For instance, the verbs " to lie " and " to lay " are confused in conversational speech to an extraordinary extent. It should be remembered that the verb to " lay " is transitive—that is, a person who lays must lay something, as a hen or a bricklayer does. " To lay *down* " is thus a physical impossibility.

Also, archaic and obsolete words should be avoided, since usage no longer requires them. We have in mind such veterans as " yclept," " whilom," " methinks," and " behest." Each has a more youthful alternative that will sound less strained.

Regarding catch-phrases, these should be used sparingly or not at all. We always feel irritated when a speech contains a sprinkling of the following : " To be or not to be," " to all intents and purposes," " more honoured in the breach than the observance," " the light, fantastic toe," " the soft impeachment " and " filthy lucre." Of course, there are many others, equally threadbare.

Then there are the Latin tags and foreign phrases. It is true that there are some abstractions that can be expressed only with difficulty in English and for which it is often advantageous to employ a foreign idiom. But generally speaking, the sprinkling of a speech with such interpolations as " a quid pro quo," " pro bono publico," and " rus in urbe," will suggest to the audience that the speaker is airing his knowledge.

Thus, it all amounts to this: If you have to make a speech, get some practice beforehand in talking at meetings and, at home, practise the art of clear and deliberate speaking.

Voice production and perfect elocution are definitely necessary to the making of a good speech. To acquire these assets, listen to a clear voice coming over the radio and proceed to practise the intonation and enunciation of the speaker.

A good lecturer using pure English is the type of voice delivery you should take as your model.

CHAPTER XI

WE will suppose that, in a week's time, you have to make a speech and the fact rather overwhelms you, seeing that you are not used to such things. As we have said, more than once, elsewhere, there is really no need to view the occasion with any apprehension. Speech-making is not nearly so much of an ordeal as you probably think.

MAKING THE PREPARATIONS.—In the first case, it will be advisable for you to study the hints offered in the chapter entitled " Speaking in Public," and having carried out as many of the suggestions given there as lie within your powers, the next thing is to settle down to planning the actual speech.

There are three ways to plan a speech. The first and best method is to go mentally over the subject on which you have to talk and merely think of what you intend to say. And, then, when the time comes, to say it.

Though this is the plan adopted by most of the best speakers, it is not one that the novice should attempt, for the very simple reason that, when the time comes, he won't say it. All the clever ideas that he planned, all the carefully built up arguments that he had prepared, all the amusing side-lights that he had in mind—all of them fly from his brain, as he stands up and gazes on the sea of faces, and everything becomes a total blank. We have experienced it all, so we know.

The second way of planning a speech is to think out all the things that have to be said and to jot down a list of headings on a slip of paper. The slip can then be used while the speech is being actually delivered. The headings will keep you on the right lines, they will help you to remember all your points, and they will not cramp your style. In other words, they will assist and not restrict you. This is usually considered as good a way as any of preparing a speech.

The third method is to sit down and write out what you intend to say from beginning to end. You can, then, take your script into a private room and go over it aloud a dozen, or, perhaps, forty times, until you have learnt much of it by heart, while the rest you can fill in by a system of paraphrasing. A glance at the paper, just before you rise to speak, will refresh your memory splendidly and, quite likely, you will be surprised and pleased at your powers of oratory, after the event.

But, if you do go to the trouble of writing out the whole of the speech, do not be tempted to read it on the great occasion. No speech that is read is as convincing as one that is delivered, while many are simply grotesque. Not so long ago we were forced to listen to a speaker who read his speech. When he came to the foot of what we imagined must been sheet No. 100, he had trouble in turning over to sheet No. 101, so there was a pause in his reading. What he said before the pause was " I am agreeably surprised," and after the pause, " to find such a large and dignified audience here to-night." The large and dignified audience laughed outright.

NOTES OF HEADINGS.—Having considered the three methods of preparing the speech, you will probably elect to follow the second, which is based on the plan of making notes of headings. Before proceeding, however, with the preparation of notes, a clear understanding of the essential component parts of a speech must be obtained. These parts may be regarded as being six in number, each following rationally from the preceding, all in direct relation to each other and the whole. They are as follows:

(1) General introduction of subject.

(2) Statement of the particular proposition which is to be expounded.

(3) The evidence in detail.

(4) The summary of evidence.

(5) Exposition of the conclusion logically to be drawn from such evidence.

(6) The appeal for support, or the " peroration."

Under these headings your notes may most conveniently be set down. Naturally, certain of the divisions are capable of further subdivision. Evidence in detail, for instance, may well have six divisions of its own, the number being mainly dependent on its bulk.

Let us suppose, for the purpose of a practical example, that you have to deliver a speech on " The Need for Prison Reform." Having acquired a fair knowledge of your subject, you come to the preparation of your notes.

First comes the question of how to open. Your introduction must be of a nature to arrest attention. Some topical or personal reference will generally achieve this end, and is the method very frequently adopted. In the present instance it will do very well.

Now, then, for the first note. Since the question is of prisons, recent police proceedings will supply a topical reference. Select a case that has received a fair amount of press comment, and under the first of the headings mentioned above, write down:

(1) John Smith, burglar. 3 years.

Having mentioned this case in opening your speech, you have to lead up to the subject of prisons. On prisons few people have very definite ideas. You may bring this home to them by asking whether they have any idea where, and to what, John Smith is going. Very good ; write as a second note, under the same heading:

Where is he going?

You will be able to enlarge on this somewhat, especially if you have made a personal visit to a prison. failing this, take your facts from reports of Royal Commissions, etc. Here is a further note to make. Under your heading of General Introduction you have, then, this:

(1) John Smith, burglar. 3 years.
    Where is he going?
    Personal visit (or report of Royal Commission, etc.)

Passing to heading (2) you have to set out your " argument " or the proposition you wish to prove. Let us suppose for the sake of the illustration that you consider that the main thing wrong with the prisons is that they are out of date. Society's attitude to criminals has changed, but parallel changes in prison buildings and, to some extent, the whole system, have lagged behind. Most of them were built in the days when it was generally accepted that the punishment should fit the crime ; now society considers generally that the punishment should fit the criminal. The prisons were built before the idea of reformation and rehabilitation of prisoners was accepted ; and prison administration, while greatly improved, is still in need of reform.

Under the heading (2), then, you will write down:
    (2) Prisons need reform.

> Punishment fit the criminal, not the crime.
> Buildings no longer suitable.
> Administration needs modernization.

So you move on to the next heading—the evidence in detail. Its quantity will be governed by the amount of time you are allowed for your speech. Certainly you will have to select ruthlessly, and even the facts that are included will have to be compressed. Naturally you will want to get as many facts in as you can ; but do not try to include everything if this means that you will not be able to do anything justice. It is better to leave out the less impressive facts and make the most of the strongest ones. And do not hesitate to weed out anything that is not strictly relevant or that does not fit in with its neighbours. There must be no suspicion of digression in your speech. It must be arranged in a logical and orderly manner, with each point leading naturally on to the next.

The evidence, of course, comes from your original notes under the heading " Facts." Take what you need, and arrange it in the most suitable order. Then write down your notes. They may be something like this:

(3) Physical overcrowding.
Poor hygiene and sanitation.
More " open prisons " needed.
Stultifying influence of unnecessary petty restrictions.
Inadequate provision of useful employment.
Lack of proper educational facilities.
Insufficient classification and segregation of prisoners.
Insufficient constructive reformatory work.

Your next heading is the summary of evidence, and this will be much briefer. For example:

(4) Overcrowding and bad conditions.
Repressive influences.
Insufficient rehabilitation.

Now you come to the logical conclusion to be drawn from all the foregoing. This is the most important part of your speech, and it must be clear and forceful. It must also anticipate possible criticisms of your argument and, if possible, disarm them. One obvious such criticism is finance ; and you might answer this in advance by pointing out that unless conditions are changed there will be more " chronic " criminals, and that crime costs the nation more than the reforms would do—that is that, far from not being able to afford to make reforms, we cannot afford not to make them.

Also you must bring out the most constructive features of your argument. In this particular example, of course, there is constructive criticism from the beginning of the speech ; but in general the way to present an argument is to criticize the present state of affairs first, pointing out the things that are wrong, and then say how they could be made better.

Bearing these points in mind, you may summarize your logical conclusions as follows:

(5) System out of date.
   Theory not put into practice.
   Need for new buildings and better adminis-
      tration.
   Cannot afford *not* to reform prisons.

Finally comes your peroration, and this is perhaps the most difficult part of your speech. Like the pre-oration, it should be striking, but in a different way: your object is to leave something in your listeners' ears—something that they will continue to remember after you have sat down. A really apt quotation makes a good peroration ; failing that, try to end with a trenchant epigram or a paradox.

In this case a possible theme for the peroration is a denial of sentimentality. Prison reformers are often labelled by their opponents as well-meaning but un-realistic persons, who do not understand the harsh facts of crime. You can anticipate this criticism and at the same time startle your listeners by declaring bluntly that you have no time for sentiment in this matter, and demand that they look at it from a strictly practical point of view. Returning indirectly to the financial angle, ask them if we can afford to allow crime to continue at its present high level. Say bluntly that there are only two ways of preventing criminals from returning to crime: one is to execute them, or at least keep them in prison until they die; the other is to reform them. At present a fatal middle course is being pursued. Modern society would not allow the extermination of all criminals, and therefore the only sane course is to try to reform them.

Put the notes for the peroration as follows:

(6) No time for sentiment.
    Exterminate or reform.

Now you have the whole pattern of your speech. Your notes will read as follows:

(1) *Pre-oration or introduction*
    John Smith, burglar. 3 years.
    Where is he going?
    Personal visit (or report of Royal Commission, etc.).

(2) *Proposition or " argument "*
    Prisons need reform.
    Punishment fit the criminal, not the crime.
    Buildings no longer suitable.
    Administration needs modernization.

(3) *Evidence in detail*
    Physical overcrowding.

Poor hygiene and sanitation.

More " open prisons " needed.

Stultifying influence of unnecessary petty restrictions.

Inadequate provision of useful employment.

Lack of proper educational facilities.

Insufficient classification and segregation of prisoners.

Insufficient constructive reformatory work.

(4) *Summary of evidence*

Overcrowding and bad conditions.

Repressive influences.

Insufficient rehabilitation.

(5) *Logical conclusions*

System out of date.

Theory not yet put into practice.

Need for new buildings and better administration.

Cannot afford not to reform prisons.

(6) *Peroration, or conclusion*

No time for sentiment.

Exterminate or reform.

Now before you go any further, try to reduce these notes to a more compact form. Put them into a kind of private shorthand, to which you alone hold the key, trying to compress ideas into single words which will be sufficient to remind you of the longer notes. For example:

(1) John Smith. 3 years. Where going? Visit.

(2) Reform. Punishment fit criminal. Building unsuitable. Administration.

(3) Overcrowding. Hygiene. "Open prisons. Restrictions. Employment. Education. Classification. Constructive work.

(4) Overcrowding. Repression. Rehabilitation.

(5) Out of date. Theory—practice. Buildings, administration. Cannot afford.

(6) Sentiment. Exterminate or reform.

The purpose of this abridged set of notes will be explained in the next chapter.

Now return to the longer notes, numbered (1) to (6). This is the framework of your speech, so before you go any further, read the notes again as critically as you can, and ask yourself (a) if they include anything that does not fit in or that could be omitted without weakening the argument ; (b) if there is any repetition or bad arrangement that is likely to cause the speech to be longer than it need be ; (c) if the existing arrangement is logical and orderly, so that each idea naturally leads to the next ; and (d) if this arrangement of your ideas really represents what you want to say.

Next turn to your original notes, and read through the facts and arguments that were not selected for inclusion. If any of these seems too important to be left out, consult the framework again to see if you can modify it to include the omitted matter.

The next step is to write out your speech. Do this quickly, without bothering to spend minutes on trying to find the best words. Speak it aloud as you write it, but do not try to revise as you go along. Do not ramble away from your headings. If you get new ideas, put them down on a separate piece of paper, for consideration after the rough draft is finished.

When your speech is finished, read it through aloud, once. Then settle down to revise it. You cannot spend too much time on this. You should polish it, rephrase it, and constantly try to improve it in every possible way. Be highly critical of it. If a word does not seem quite right, try to find a better one. You will find synonyms in any dictionary, and many more in Roget's *Thesaurus*. Consider each argument, and see if you can find a clearer and more forceful way of expressing your points.

When at last your revision is complete, put the speech away for a day or so. Then get it out and again read it aloud, and make any further revisions that seem necessary. There will be some!

Now time the speech, allowing for pauses. If it is too long, cut it ruthlessly. Do not keep telling yourself that if you cut it down you will not do justice to your subject. Remember that you will have left your strongest arguments to the end, and they are not going to have much effect if half your audience has gone to sleep before they are delivered.

When you have got your speech down to the allotted length—a little less is better than a little more—polish it again. You can go on polishing at intervals right up until the time has come for you to make the speech, and after each revision it will look more and more like a finished article.

Finally take out your set of abridged notes and compare them with the speech. Modify them to take into account the revisions you have made. This check will serve the additional purpose of showing whether you have kept to the logical and orderly arrangement of your ideas.

The next step is to prepare for the delivery, and this will be described in the following chapter.

CHAPTER XII

SOME wise person has put it on record that the way to deliver a speech is to stand up, to speak up and, then, to shut up. Actually, this is excellent advice which quite a number of even old-hands might take to heart.

To deal with the question of your pose first: When you rise, stand perfectly erect, but not stiffly. Do not, for instance, loll on to the table or twist yourself over a chair-back. Put your hands behind you or hold them together in front. There are occasions when it will not matter if they go into your pockets, but if you do this with them, do not jingle your money. Above all, do not use your hands for fidgeting with things. We know one after-dinner speaker who always forms a square on the table with forks and spoons. All his friends wonder what he would do if a waiter deprived him of these articles.

If, when you rise, you feel nervous, a good plan is to deflate the lungs, then to take in a full breath of air and to expel it slowly—all, of course, without anyone being able to notice what you are doing. This will put more than the usual supply of oxygen into your blood, and it will have the effect of steadying the nerves. Try it and you will be surprised.

We know a staunch teetotaller who always drinks a glass of wine just before he has to rise. He tells us that it gives him the necessary "kick" for making him equal to anything. He salves his conscience by saying it is medicine. Certainly, a glass of wine does serve to loosen the tongue, but it may cloud the brain and muddle your thought.

STARTING OFF.—Your first words will consist of whatever formula is appropriate, " Mr. Chairman, Gentlemen," or " Ladies and Gentlemen," etc. The mere fact of having to begin in this way is useful because it gives you a chance of making a start without effort. Thereafter you will continue with your subject matter. If it is a business meeting, your speech will be taken up with the statements that you are required to make, so your course should not be difficult. Nor should there be any trouble in deciding what to say, if you are making a speech as an official at a social or other club. The business in hand will supply your subject matter. It is when you are called upon to speak at a dinner and reply to some toast about which you happen to know very little that you may be starved for ideas, especially if all the previous speakers have stolen your thunder.

Of course, there are ways out of difficulties such as these. One plan is to acknowledge the honour that you feel has been conferred on you by being entrusted with whatever toast or subject has been forced on you. Then, you can continue by confessing complete ignorance of the whole matter, and if you play your part well, it will be possible to convulse your audience with laughter. And, do not forget that it is not terribly difficult to provoke laughter after a dinner. Your listeners are wonderfully considerate.

But, if you think of striking a humorous note, try to do it off your own bat, so to speak. If you must bring in a joke, and there is no reason why you should not, see to it that it has some bearing on your utterances. Too often, a speaker introduces a joke by saying, " That reminds me of a story I heard the other night at the club." Thereafter, everybody is left wondering what it was that reminded the speaker of the story, with the consequence that the psychology of the whole speech is ruined.

Do not feel that you must speak for a given number of minutes. If you have said all that you have in mind, nobody will object if you sit down before the clock has ticked off your allotted span of time. In fact, you are more likely to be thanked. At the outside, ten minutes should be the most you are on your feet, unless you are an important personage, such as the chairman. Naturally, he may have a good deal to say and, therefore, he must be given more freedom.

What you say is important, but how you say it is equally so. Make it a rule to speak slowly and be deliberate, but do not be a hesitater—one of those people who pause for such a long while that the audience begins to wonder whether anything has happened. Enunciate every word clearly and fully. Above all, do not slur or clip your words, but pronounce every syllable fully. If you want to be a hundred per cent. audible, form your words on the tip of your tongue against your front teeth. It is the people who speak down in their throats that are difficult to hear.

When you have dealt with all your facts, make some sort of a conclusion to your remarks, and then sit down.

CHAPTER XIII

DEBATING SOCIETIES

TO-DAY, there are more young men and women who are politically inclined than there have ever been in the past. Moreover, the ranks are being continually added to by newcomers who want to take their share in the government of the country.

To the credit of these young men and women, it can be truthfully said that the majority of them are anxious to make themselves politically efficient. In no way is this more noticeable than in their desire to become, what has been called, articulate in public.

For those who wish to master the art of platform speaking, there is no better method than the formation of small, more or less informal, debating classes. Half a dozen friends can easily get together and meet, in rotation, at their respective homes one night a week, but they must first enlist the services of somebody who has ability as a speaker and who will take on the rôle of teacher.

The teacher, at the outset, will act as chairman and he will use his tact and experience to assist the more nervous beginners. At the first meeting, he should give or read a short address on the principles of good speaking. This may well be followed by calling upon each member to speak for, say, two minutes on any subject.

Generally, a request for some personal reminiscences elicits the most ready response. Those whose nervousness is so great that they cannot bring themselves to speak at all coherently may be given one or two short passages to read, at intervals, until they gain some slight confidence in themselves.

After each little speech or effort at correct reading, the teacher should offer a few critical remarks. These must not be too destructive, nor yet too effusive but at the same time they ought to reflect a certain measure of truth.

At a few subsequent meetings, the members of the class should be set, more and more, to giving their opinions on controversial topics, and these opinions should be criticised by their audience.

At, say, the fourth or fifth meeting, the chairman should give a short address on the component parts of a speech and the system of arranging the notes for a speech. When these methods have been assimilated, it will be found interesting to devote about half the time of a meeting to prepared speeches, and the remaining half to a short debate on some topic proposed and decided upon by vote.

After this stage, the evolution of the class into a debating circle, pure and simple, will be almost inevitable: and when, by general opinion, the need for the criticizing system is no longer felt, no time should be lost in constituting, with correct rules and officers, a proper debating society.

THE CONSTITUTION OF A DEBATING SOCIETY.—Such a society should have the following officers:

(1) A President or Chairman.

(2) A Vice-President or Vice-Chairman.

(3) A Secretary and Treasurer (if desired, these offices may be held separately or jointly.)

(4) A Committee should be formed of all the officers and, at least, an equal number of ordinary members.

The President, or the Vice-Chairman, when the former is absent, will take the chair at all meetings.

The Secretary has charge of all the society's correspondence, is responsible that the minutes are properly recorded, and it is his duty to arrange debates with other clubs, and to inform members whenever meetings are to be held.

The Treasurer has charge of members' subscriptions, sees that they are paid and he keeps the accounts of the society generally. On him rests the responsibility of paying all outgoings and of keeping the receipts.

The Committee selects subjects for debate, the speakers to open in the affirmative and the negative, and arranges the programme for all the society's activities. It decides on all questions arising within the society, and is generally responsible for the drawing up of the code of rules.

In all of the more enlightened societies, there is a desire that its members should obtain not only practice in speaking but, also, in the conduct of meetings. Therefore, facilities are given for every member to act the part of chairman occasionally. The actual chairman opens the proceedings and then vacates the chair in favour of the member whose turn it is to fill the office on that evening. Naturally, this is only done when the society meets privately and visitors are not present.

At an ordinary meeting, the chairman will first dispose of the business of the meeting by having the minutes read and approved and then he will deal with any other matters. This he should do with as little delay as possible, since the majority of those present will be anxious to enter on the debate.

Then, the chairman will state the subject for discussion and call upon the openers, in turn. In open discussion, it is usually the rule to allow each member an agreed time to speak, and to speak once only, although a member may rise at any time on " a point of order."

When the time is up, or no more speakers are forthcoming, the chairman should call upon the opener, or if there were two openers, upon both of them, in turn, to make a short reply to the criticism advanced.

The motion should, then, be put to the meeting and a vote taken by a show of hands. The result of the voting should, then, be announced clearly by the chairman and recorded by the secretary.

Members should endeavour to speak on all occasions, since practice is absolutely necessary for progress. They should, also, realise that some knowledge is needed before speaking can be intelligent: therefore every subject set down for debate should be studied beforehand.

CHAPTER XIV

READY-MADE SPEECHES

In this section, a number of set speeches is given at full length. It is hardly intended that they should be delivered, on any appropriate occasion, word for word.

In almost every case, they will be immeasurably improved by the addition of some reference or allusion to actual facts. Such facts, of course, cannot be given in these pages. They are personal or private details which will be suggested by the occasion and the moment.

It should be recognised that, with slight changes, almost every speech given here will serve for several occasions other than that mentioned. Thus, the collection has unlimited uses.

THE QUEEN

This toast is almost always proposed by the chairman or host. It always heads the toast list ; and, as smoking is not permitted until this toast has been given, the chairman is expected to propose it as soon as possible after the last course of the meal has been finished.

The proposer is not required to make a speech. He simply rises and utters the time-honoured formula :

Ladies and Gentlemen (*or* Gentlemen)—the Queen!

Immediately after this toast the chairman should announce:

Ladies and Gentlemen (*or* Gentlemen), you may smoke.

HER MAJESTY'S FORCES
(Usually proposed by the Chairman)

Hints.—Obviously there must be a patriotic ring about this speech, but it should not be overdone and there must not be any suspicion of bombast. The proper note to strike is quiet, sober sincerity, without any striving after effect. If the proposer himself has served in the Forces, a little gentle humour may be introduced as relief, but it must not be either pompous or patronizing. If the proposer has never served in the Forces, humour is best avoided, and gratitude and respect should be expressed.

SPECIMEN

Gentlemen,—I do not think that any sailor, soldier, or airman is going to take me to task when I say that we are a peace-loving nation. Fighting is not one of our national sports. Our only conception of war is self-defence.

It is often said that it takes two to make a quarrel. I suppose there is some truth in this. A quarrelsome person has to find someone to quarrel with, and his victim is not bound to defend himself. In this sense we must plead guilty to having taken part in some long and hard quarrels in modern times. But it is worth remembering that if we had not been, in this extreme sense, such a quarrelsome nation, we should not be a nation at all today. We have a clean record. We have done everything possible to avert wars, and we have taken up arms only when our national existence and freedom have been threatened.

For a people who are so slow and reluctant to fight we have fought pretty well. I say " we," for modern war is total war, in which everyone is involved. But although the character of war has changed, let us not forget that the grim business of fighting is still done by the Fighting Forces. I do not mean to belittle the Home Front when I say that civilians, whatever their own efforts, are in the eternal debt of the men who have gone out to grapple with the enemy on land, at sea, and in the air.

Nor is this just a wartime debt. Our Forces not only win wars ; they prevent them. Whatever contributions our statesmen and diplomats have made to world peace—and I think they have made many—they would have been powerless without the backing of our Armed Forces.

Our Forces are not numerically large, and they have won wars against heavy odds. Their great strength, I think, lies mainly in their efficiency and especially in their high morale. Sane discipline is tempered with individual self-discipline, and it is this latter quality that has made our Servicemen our finest Ambassadors in every part of the world to which duty has taken them.

The toast is to Her Majesty's Forces, and I do not want to discriminate among the different Services that together protect our nation and our freedom. Our debt is the same to them all—and to them as a whole, not in parts.

Gentlemen, I give you the toast of Her Majesty's Forces ; and I have pleasure in coupling with it the name of our distinguished guest, ——.

REPLY TO THE TOAST OF HER MAJESTY'S FORCES

Hints.—The reply will be made by a serving member of one of the Forces. Whatever Service he belongs to, he should stress the basic unity of the three Forces.

SPECIMEN

Mr. Chairman, Gentlemen,—The task of replying to this most generous toast fills me with both pride and alarm. Of the two, I think the alarm is stronger. In the Army we try to keep in step, but we do not speak with one voice. Heaven forbid! But now I am called upon to speak not only for the whole of the British Army, but for the Royal Navy and the Royal Air Force as well. The task is too heavy ; and I must ask you to allow me to speak simply for myself.

The first thing I want to say is that while I am dismayed at having to reply to this toast, I warmly support the form in which it has been proposed. You have honoured the three Services as one whole, and that, I think, is how they should be considered. Of course each Service has its own traditions, its own customs, and perhaps even its own language ; but at heart we are pretty well at one.

I do not want to suggest that there is no such thing as inter-Service rivalry. On the contrary, it is very keen—and, I think, a good thing. Co-operation and competition are sometimes regarded as opposites, but in the Services they stimulate each other. And as for the Service rivalry—well believe me, the rivalry between the Army and the Navy or Air Force is quite tame compared with the rivalry between two of our crack regiments!

On behalf of Her Majesty's Forces, I thank you.

THE ROYAL NAVY
(Usually proposed by the Chairman)

Hints.—Again the keynote is sober patriotism. If the proposer of the toast is serving or has served in the Army or R.A.F., he can brighten up his speech with some friendly inter-Service chaffing ; but he should not overdo this, and ought to end on a note of sincere respect. If the proposer is not an ex-Serviceman, he should not try to make jokes at the expense of the Service. Historical allusions can be brought in, but should be used sparingly.

SPECIMEN

Gentlemen,—I now have the honour to propose the toast of the " Silent Service "—the Royal Navy. It may well be silent, for it has no need to boast aloud. Its deeds have always spoken for themselves. From the days of the Armada to the Battle of the Atlantic, it has held the supremacy of the sea.

The task of our Navy has been a heavy one. Not only has it had to guard our long island coastline, but it has had to protect our vital sea routes and keep them open for shipping in all the great oceans of the world. As the senior Service it has a great tradition ; but at the same time it has always shown itself strikingly progressive. For many centuries naval warfare meant either ships against ships or ships against shore batteries. In modern times ships have been attacked by two new weapons of deadly striking power—one from above and one from below. Together they constituted a challenge to the very existence of the Navy— and, therefore, a challenge to the safety of our island home. Our Navy met this challenge and triumphed over it. In the Second World War it protected our lifelines when we were hardest pressed. It rescued our Army from Dunkirk ; it supported the R.A.F. in the Battle of Britain ; and it led the way to the liberation of Europe on D-Day. Its losses were heavy ; but without it we could not have won the war. It has continued to move with the times, and if new weapons are levelled against it in the future, I am confident that it will find the answer to these as well.

Our ships are the finest in the world. But ships alone do not make a Navy. In the old days we spoke of ships of oak and hearts of oak. Nowadays our ships are of steel ; and it is not too much to say that the staunchness of our sailors has evolved in a like manner with their ships. Nothing but iron courage and nerves of steel can stand the strain of naval warfare today.

Our Navy is a force of which we can be more justly proud today than ever before. I ask you, gentlemen, to drink to the health of the Royal Navy, and I couple with the toast the name of ——

REPLY TO THE TOAST OF THE ROYAL NAVY
SPECIMEN

Mr. Chairman, Gentlemen,—I must apologize for standing up and breaking one of the naval traditions which has just been warmly praised. I have been reminded that the Service to which I have the honour of belonging is famous for its silence ; and such a compliment deserves a more appropriate reply than a speech.

Nor, indeed, is there anything I can say, beyond expressing my thanks for the most cordial way in which you have received this toast. I would add only this: service in the British Navy is a great privilege as well as a responsibility. In playing our part in the defence of the country we have always known that we have had the trust and confidence of the people behind us. This means a lot to us ; and, come what may, I promise you that we shall continue to try to be worthy of this trust. Gentlemen, on behalf of the Navy, I thank you.

THE MAYOR AND CORPORATION

Hints.—This toast is generally proposed at a civic dinner or other function, where the Mayor will be known personally by many of those present. A personal element should therefore be introduced into the speech—for example, if it is known that the Mayor is a keen golfer, some humorous reference should be made to the fact.

SPECIMEN

Mr. Chairman, Gentlemen,—I am happy to have the duty of proposing the toast of the Mayor and Corporation. Most of us, I am afraid, are in the habit of taking the Corporation for granted. What is worse, on the few occasions when we do think about it, our thoughts are not always kindly. We remember the Corporation when there are elections—and then, of course, the Corporation remembers us ; and we remember it especially twice every year, when we get the demands for our rates. Otherwise we seem to forget that the Corporation exists. My only defence for this apparently ungrateful attitude is that it shows, far better than any words could do, just how efficiently the Corporation does its work. It never lets us down.

But although we may take the Corporation for granted, the same does not apply to the Mayor. He is not the sort of man you can ignore. He is a personality—a character. He leaves his mark on everything he does. If you do not believe me, I invite you to go up to the golf course and have a look at the bunker behind the green at the fifteenth hole. There you will see what a worshipful niblick did three months ago.

But I am not being fair. Our Mayor, as you know, is tireless in the performance of his many public duties, and we have every reason to be grateful to him.

Both he and all the members of the Corporation labour unstintingly for the good of the community. They set a magnificent example in local government— and I only wish that the Governments of the world were in similar hands.

Gentlemen, I ask you to drink to the health of our Mayor and Corporation.

INTRODUCING THE CANDIDATE AT AN ELECTION MEETING
(Made by the Chairman)

Hints.—The difficulty in making a speech involving political considerations is not so much in the subject matter as in handling the audience. When you make a social speech or propose a convivial toast, you will find generally that your listeners will meet you in a friendly spirit ; but whenever you have to touch on politics in public, you may be sure that at least a section of your audience will be hostile, and probably vocally so. In preparing your speech you must keep this danger well in mind, and try to avoid including anything that will provoke awkward questions or facetious remarks intended to ridicule what you say.

In introducing a candidate you are not expected to go into details of his policy—that is the candidate's task. But your speech is important, because if it is properly prepared and delivered you can get the audience into the right spirit for listening to what the candidate has to say. Naturally your speech should be largely personal, but do not make the mistake of giving the candidate extravagant praise, which might provoke derision and therefore cause embarrassment.

SPECIMEN

Ladies and Gentlemen,—As chairman of this meeting I have the pleasure of introducing Mr. —— as candidate to represent the interests of this Borough in Parliament. As you know, he is the representative of the —— Party ; and as you will have guessed, if you did not already know, I too am a supporter of that Party. I believe in its principles and its policy, and I am convinced that if it is returned to power at this Election—as I am sure it will be—every member of the community will benefit.

But I am not going to talk politics, or to try to anticipate our candidate's speech. You have come to hear him, and I am not going to waste your time with a long introduction. All I want to say is that Mr. —— is, in my opinion, admirably fitted to represent this Borough, not only because his politics are sound—and they are very sound, as you will soon find out—but because he is a man of great personal integrity and ability. I commend him to you, ladies and gentlemen, and I trust you will give him the good hearing he deserves.

USEFUL QUOTATIONS

He serves his party best, who serves the country best.—*Hayes.*

There is no perfecter endowment in man than political virtue.—*Plutarch.*

Can anybody remember when times were not hard and money not scarce?—*Emerson.*

We cannot eat the fruit while the tree is in blossom. —*Disraeli.*

Work is the great cure of all maladies and miseries that ever beset mankind.—*Carlyle*.

There's dignity in labour.—*Swain*.

PROPOSING THE ADOPTION OF A CANDIDATE FOR AN ELECTION

Hints.—Candidates for Elections are adopted at meetings of the local Party, so here the issue is more personal than political. However, a candidate is adopted more for his political ability than for his personal qualities, and the speaker who proposes his adoption should base his case on this.

SPECIMEN

Mr. Chairman, Ladies and Gentlemen.—I have the agreeable task of proposing the adoption of Mr. —— as our candidate for the coming General Election. I am not going to support my proposal by drawing from my personal knowledge of Mr. ——, because the matter is too important for sentiment. We are all agreed that it is our task to choose the best possible candidate—that is, the candidate most likely to win the Election and to represent us in the way we would wish after he has been elected. I think that Mr. —— is entirely suitable on both counts. He has been very frank about his opinions on those points in the Party programme that concern us most, and I think you will agree that his views are entirely sound. He is a man of considerable political knowledge and experience, and he has that high degree of common sense necessary for a politician in dealing with those problems and issues that inevitably arise after the Election is over.

You all know that this is by no means an easy constituency and only a strong candidate can have any hope of winning it. I think that Mr. —— has just the qualities that will appeal to the electorate. His public record is excellent, he has a most pleasant personality, he is an excellent speaker, and he impresses people as a man who will get things done. And I am sure that when he is elected he will get them done, too. It is therefore with every confidence that I propose that he should be formally adopted as our candidate.

OUR MEMBER OF PARLIAMENT

Hints.—The toast to the local M.P. may be proposed at a purely Party gathering or at a function where the audience is more general. In the latter case the speaker should steer clear of political controversy, for the proposal of a toast should be so worded that the toast itself will be readily acceptable by the whole audience.

SPECIMEN

Ladies and Gentlemen,—It is with great pleasure that I rise to propose the toast of our Member of Parliament. This is not a political function, and I am not going to make a political speech. Indeed, I am not going to make a speech at all, for I am sure that after the last stormy session at Westminster, Mr. —— has heard enough speeches to last him until the end of the recess. All I want to say is this. Whatever our Member has said in the House of Commons—and he may be surprised to know how closely we read his speeches —he has never forgotten the interests of his constituents. On several occasions he has spoken up on our behalf, even at the risk of making himself unpopular with the Party to which he belongs ; and ever since he was elected he has, I know, personally investigated every request and complaint that he has received from a constituent. His presence with us today is one more example of his concern with local affairs, and when he next presents himself to the electorate, whether we put him in again or cast him into the political wilderness, he may rest assured that the efforts he has made on our behalf as a community will have been both recognized and appreciated.

Ladies and Gentlemen, I give you the toast of Mr. ——, our M.P.

THE LADIES

Hints.—This toast is usually proposed by the youngest bachelor in the company, and the spirit of this choice should be reflected in his speech. It should be light-hearted but, of course, flattering to the fair sex. Humour is naturally desirable, but the speaker should exercise particular care to ensure that his jokes are in good taste. If a joke seems only a shade doubtful, it is better left out.

SPECIMEN

Gentlemen.—The task of proposing this toast has been given to me because I happen to be the youngest bachelor here tonight. I do not know the origin of this custom, but I imagine it must be because the youngest is the least likely to be a confirmed bachelor, and his single state is probably not due to any lack of appreciation of the opposite sex. In my own case I may as well admit that I am full of appreciation. The ladies here tonight have only a poor speaker to extol their charms, but they could not find a more devoted admirer.

I hope you will not think that because I am single, I know nothing about the ladies. I have not, of course, the same concentrated experience of a married man, but no doubt that will come later. Meanwhile I am steadily enlarging my knowledge of the fair sex in general—at least, to the extent that they will allow me. And every enlargement of my knowledge adds further to my admiration. The fact is, gentlemen, that the time seems to be approaching when I shan't be able to keep away from them!

We sometimes hear talk, even in these modern times, of the so-called equality of women, as though it were something to be argued about. I am neither a social historian nor a prophet, but I venture to suggest that such a thing as equality between the sexes has never existed and never will exist. Women have never been our equals ; they have always been vastly superior to us. There would be more sense in talking about equality for men, but personally I hope it never comes to that. Let the ladies remain as different, as feminine, and as irresistible as they are now.

I ask you to join me in drinking to the health of all our charmers. Gentlemen—the Ladies!

USEFUL QUOTATIONS

Nature intended that woman should be her master-piece—*Lessing*.

O woman, lovely woman, nature made thee
To temper man ; we had been brutes without you.
—*Thomas Otway*.

I for one venerate a petticoat.—*Lord Byron*.

The most beautiful object in the world, it will be allowed, is a beautiful woman.—*Lord Macaulay*.

Man has his will ; but woman has her way.—*O. W. Holmes*.

OUR GUESTS

Hints.—The specimen given below will need to be adapted to the nature of the function and especially to the guests who have been invited to attend. The proposer should include in his speech some complimentary allusions to the more prominent guests—including, of course, the guest who has been chosen to reply to the toast.

SPECIMEN

Ladies and Gentlemen,—It is my privilege to propose the health of our guests. It is an easy task, and requires few words and no formality from me ; for most of our guests are not strangers. I hope that by the time they leave they will all think of themselves as our friends.

Some of our guests have travelled quite a long way to be with us tonight, and I know I am expressing the general opinion when I say how much we appreciate the compliment they have paid us in spending the evening with us. I only hope that they will not regret their kindness. I am reminded that the late George Bernard Shaw was once a guest at a social function and was asked afterwards what the company was like. " Terrible," he replied. " I should have been bored stiff if I hadn't been there." I hope none of our guests will think this worth quoting when they are asked the same question.

We are pleased to see with us (insert the allusions to prominent guests).

Finally, I want to say how much pleasure the presence of all our guests has given to us, and to express the hope that we shall have many opportunities of seeing more of them in the future and getting to know them better.

Gentlemen, I give you the toast of—our guests

THE BRIDE AND BRIDEGROOM

Hints.—This toast, which is usually proposed by an old friend of the bride, should be brief and tactful. The proposer should remember that the bride and groom are probably embarrassed, and he should not try to get cheap laughs at their expense.

SPECIMEN

Ladies and Gentlemen,—I have a happy duty to perform on this happy occasion. I am going to ask you all to drink to the health and happiness of the bride and groom. It is an especially happy task because I can perform it with such confidence. Both of them look the picture of health, and their happiness is beyond concealment.

Marriage has sometimes been called a lottery, but I am sure there is no gamble about this match. Both the bride and groom took a peek in advance at the winning numbers before they chose their tickets. Of course I could have told the groom that he had found a winner right from the start, for I have known the bride since she was a sweet and lovable child, and watched her become sweeter and more lovable as she grew up. But the groom wisely did not ask my opinion, and nor did the bride. I hope they will forgive me if I give it now, and say that if ever a marriage was made in heaven, this is it.

No one ever forgets his wedding day, and the young couple will look back on this day with sweet memories as the years pass. I doubt if their memories will include my speech, so I shall detain you no further. Ladies and Gentlemen, I ask you to drink to the health and happiness of the bride and groom.

USEFUL QUOTATIONS

Thy wife is a constellation of virtues; she's the moon, and thou art the man in the moon.—*Congreve*.

Of all actions of a man's life, his marriage does least concern other people ; yet of all actions of our life 'tis most meddled with by other people.—*Table Talk*.

No woman should marry a teetotaller, or a man who does not smoke.—*R. L. Stevenson*.

REPLY TO THE TOAST OF THE BRIDE AND BRIDEGROOM

Hints.—This speech, which is always made by the bridegroom, can be very brief. No one expects a flow of oratory from a man who has just got married, and it is enough if he simply voices his thanks. Should he want to make a longer speech, he will naturally say how fortunate he considers himself, but he should not give a long list of the bride's qualities ; nor should he forget to mention his appreciation of the kindness shown to him by her parents. It is usual for the bridegroom's speech to end with the toast to the bridesmaids.

SPECIMEN

Ladies and Gentlemen,—My wife and I—I must get used to this way of speaking—thank you all most sincerely for your kind wishes. I am sure you will excuse me from making a long speech, and will understand that at the moment I am quite incapable of making one. I don't need to tell you that I think I am the luckiest man in the world, and that my only ambition is to be worthy of my luck. I must add that today I have not only gained the best wife any man could have, but I have also acquired an extra mother and father. No parents could have been kinder to a man bent on stealing their daughter.

Before I sit down, I must ask you to join me in drinking to the health of the very charming ladies who have supported my wife in her ordeal—if that is the right word. Ladies and Gentlemen—to the Bridesmaids!

USEFUL QUOTATIONS

The most precious possession that ever comes to a man in this world is a woman's heart.—*Holland.*

OUR OPPONENTS (CRICKET)

Hints.—Of course sportsmanship is the keynote of this toast, with emphasis on friendly rivalry and the fact that the game is more important than the result. If your own side has won, make little of the success, mention any luck you may have had, and dwell on the difficulty your team experienced before it could claim the victory. If your side has lost, do not bemoan the absence of your best players or claim that you were unlucky ; say that the better team won, and that you hope to get your revenge next time.

Often the convention is for the toast to be proposed by the captain of the winning team and answered by his opposite number ; but sometimes the toast is proposed by the captain of the home team, irrespective of the result of the match.

SPECIMEN

Gentlemen,—I have the greatest pleasure in proposing to you the toast of our opponents. I know you will agree with me that we had an exellent game. As it happened, we managed to scrape a win, and on paper it may look a comfortable victory. In fact, as you all know, our opponents gave us some very uncomfortable moments, and the score-book flatters us. Of course I am glad we won ; but I am still gladder that we had such a good game. Our opponents were not only keen and able players—their fielding, in particular, was a lesson to us—but they showed themselves fine sportsmen. It is not for the result that we shall remember this game so much as the spirit in which it was played.

The next time we meet we shall try to win again—although I don't mind admitting that we expect at least as hard a struggle as we had today, but whatever the result, we know in advance that we shall have a good game, played in the spirit in which cricket should always be played.

Gentlemen, I give you the toast of our opponents, the —— (name of club), coupled with the name of their captain, A—— B——.

USEFUL QUOTATIONS

Always play fair, and think fair ; and if you win don't crow about it ; and if you lose don't fret—*Eden Phillpotts.*

Success is sweet : the sweeter if long delayed and attained through manifold struggles and defeats—*Leigh Hunt, " Table Talk."*

REPLY TO THE TOAST OF OUR OPPONENTS (CRICKET)
Hints.—See under Our Opponents (Cricket).

SPECIMEN

Gentlemen,—On behalf of a very chastened team, I wish to thank you for your most cordial toast. We have been soundly beaten, and I had no intention to try to make excuses ; but I did not expect to hear excuses made for us. You are too generous in your victory, and I can only reply by saying that the better team won, and we know it. But it is a great comfort to hear that you do not consider your afternoon was entirely wasted, or that you might have done better at

the nets. Whatever faults there were in our play—
and I know there were plenty—we tried our hardest
to give you a good game. The simple fact was that you
were too good for us. But we enjoyed the match tre-
mendously, and it is a relief to hear that you got some
pleasure out of it.

I must thank you also for the way you have enter-
tained us, providing us with a magnificent tea (and
dinner) which we did little to deserve.

According to my memory, a fixture has been
arranged for a return match in six weeks' time. Then
we shall have the pleasure of offering you our hos-
pitality—which I am afraid will hardly equal yours—
and, we hope, of avenging today's defeat. It may seem
boastful to ı ·e this suggestion, after our performance
today ; but like most cricketers, we never know when
we are beāten, and the next time we take the field
against you we shall be more determined than ever.
Anyway, whatever the result, I share your knowledge
that we are going to have another good, sporting game.

On behalf of the —— (name of club), gentlemen, I
thank you.

SUCCESS TO THE CLUB (LAWN TENNIS)

Hints.—This is a common toast at the annual club
dinner, and is generally proposed by the chairman.
The speech should include tributes to the secretary
(who will reply to the toast) and other officials, and
also to the captain ; but unless there has been an
exceptionally outstanding player, it is advisable not
to single out individual members of the team for

special mention, for obvious reasons. However, any success by a club member in representative or other such matches should be mentioned.

SPECIMEN

Ladies and Gentlemen,—In proposing the toast of success to the club, I think I can do no better than express the hope that the club will enjoy as much success next season as it did during the season that has just ended. In only one respect can I hope for something better—and that, of course, is the weather. But I am not going to stress this point too much ; because although the weather could be better than it was this year, I need hardly remind you that it has sometimes been a good deal worse.

I think I am voicing the general opinion when I say that we have all had a most enjoyable season. On the courts there was never a dull moment. There were some moments, indeed (here follow with any amusing incidents that occurred during the season).

We have put up a good show in club matches, and our own tournaments have been more successful than ever. I am sure you will all join me in congratulating our new champions, —— —— and —— ——, and in the doubles —— —— and —— ——, —— —— and —— ——, and —— —— and —— ——.

We are sorry that we are losing two of our oldest members, who are moving to another district. Both —— —— and —— —— have served the club well, and we wish them every success in the game in the future. A happier matter is the admission of several youngsters who, I hope, will shortly be putting their parents in their place.

Whatever doubts I might have about the future of the club, of one thing I am sure ; next season we shall again be delighted by the appearance of our ladies in new fashions which, in mixed doubles, have the effect of making it difficult for the men to keep their eye on the ball. Whenever a new costume appears, I always hear powerful arguments to show that its whole purpose is to enable the wearer to move more freely and play a better game. It would be churlish of me to suggest that this might not be the whole reason, and I am sure I should be doing a disservice to my own sex if I said anything that might deter the ladies from enchanting our eyes as they have done in the past.

Finally, I want to pay my tribute to the club officials, and especially our energetic secretary, who have worked so hard so that we could play.

Ladies and Gentlemen, I give you the toast—Success to the club!

USEFUL QUOTATIONS

They also serve who also stand and wait.—*Milton*.
The faith they have in tennis and tall stockings,
Short blistered breeches.   *—Shakespeare*.
See also under Our Opponents (Cricket).

CHAIRMAN'S REPORT AT AN ANNUAL GENERAL MEETING

Hints.—This speech will include a brief review of the year's trading, and the Chairman is required only to give the facts. Any attempt at oratory would be out of place, but the Chairman may wish to give his opinion about the future of the Company.

SPECIMEN

Gentlemen,—Before we proceed to the business of this meeting, I have two matters of personal interest to mention. The first is a sad one. I must remind you of the loss we have sustained through the death of Mr. —— ——. As you know Mr. —— was one of our oldest Directors, and he served us well in good times and bad. We shall feel the loss of his wise counsel and shrewd foresight ; and still more we shall miss a loyal and sincere friend. On this occasion I should like to record our deep sympathy for his family. (Pause.)

The other personal matter to which I must draw your attention is of a happier kind. It is that Mr. —— ——, who has been a Director for —— years, has been elected a Member of Parliament. I am sure that you will want me, on behalf of the meeting, to congratulate Mr. —— most warmly. Happily the nation's gain will not be our loss ; for although Mr. —— will have less time to spend on the Company's affairs, he is remaining on the Board and will continue to give us the benefit of his considerable experience and ability.

Last year's trading, as you will see, was satisfactory from every point of view. Our net profits amounted to £——, which represents an increase of £—— on the previous year. Provision for taxation required £—— (as compared with £—— the previous year). With the amount brought forward there is available for distribution the sum of £——.

A final dividend of 50 per cent., making 65 per cent. (less tax) on Ordinary Share Capital is proposed. This will absorb £——. After appropriations the carry forward is £——.

Our total reserves, including capital reserves, now amount to £——. This represents an increase of £——.

(Now follow with a review of the past year's history relating to buildings, plant, new projects, exports, etc.)

You will see that the volume of our business has risen by over 20 per cent. It is difficult to forecast business conditions in the coming year ; but provided that the supply o᷍ raw materials is undisturbed, and that prices remain at their present level, there is every reason to believe that our profits will be at least maintained and possibly increased.

During the last year much modernization has been carried out, and in spite of the considerable outlay it is our belief that this has already proved an excellent investment. Further modernization still awaits to be done, and it is our intention to continue this policy as circumstances permit.

Our employees now number ——. Apart from the normal replacements, there have been comparatively few changes of staff during the year. We give a lot of thought to the well-being of our staff, and our Welfare Department has provided (give details). There is a healthy team spirit among the employees of the Company, and I am sure you will wish to join with me in expressing our appreciation of the devotion and loyalty of our staff.

PROPOSAL FOR THE ELECTION OF A DIRECTOR OF A COMPANY
(Usually made by the Chairman)

SPECIMEN

Gentlemen,—I have the agreeable task of proposing that a Directorship be awarded to Mr. ——. As you know Mr. —— has served the Company for —— years, and during the last —— years he has held the position of Works Manager. To say that he has carried out his duties efficiently would be an understatement ; for he has given the Company not only the benefit of his considerable ability, but a rare devotion and personal enthusiasm for his work. Mr. —— has shown considerable initiative as well as executive powers, and I am convinced that it is in the best interests of the Company that he should now be rewarded with a Directorship.

TRADE UNION SECRETARY'S REPORT OF THE YEAR'S WORK

Hints.—A secretary's job is to state the facts clearly and concisely, and no special eloquence is required for this speech. The subject matter will, of course, depend upon the circumstances, and the following specimen may have to be considerably adapted.

SPECIMEN

Mr. Chairman and Gentlemen,—The activities of the Union on behalf of its members during the last year are well known to you, and I do not need to go over them again here. I have, however, a few matters to report. One is that our membership has increased by ——, bringing the total up to ——. This, of course, is the highest number we have ever had in the Union. In the course of the year we held —— meetings, at which the attendances were slightly higher than in the previous year. Our social activities have been increased, and as a result of their popularity it is intended that they should be further expanded next year.

You will have seen the general state of our finances from the copies of the balance sheet that have been circulated. There are one or two items, however, on which you would probably like a few words of explanation. The expenditure on —— was necessitated by ——, etc.

I do not need to make any comment on the matter of ——, which was the most important of our activities during the year. As you know, the Union's just claims in this matter were completely met in the end, and our thanks are due to Mr. —— and Mr. ——, who carried out the negotiations for us with great energy and perseverance. The matter of —— is still pending, as you know; and I expect that this will be discussed later during the meeting.

SPEECH AT A TRADE UNION MEETING

Hints.—The specimen below is a fairly typical speech that may be adapted for many different sets of circumstances. The speaker should not try to be over-eloquent, but should simply state his points clearly, briefly, and bluntly.

SPECIMEN

Mr. Chairman and Comrades,—There seems to be general agreement among us that we should take vigorous action in the matter of ——, which was sprung on us unexpectedly by the ——. The only question on which we are not agreed is what form this action should take.

My first point is that our action must be swift and vigorous, or else there will be danger of an unofficial strike. Please do not misunderstand me when I call this a danger. I am not using the word in the sense that it is often used in certain sections of the Press. I mean that an unofficial strike would be a danger to us. It would undermine the power of the Union, and that must be avoided at all costs.

My second point is that our action, although swift, should not be hasty. Now I know that the —— has forced this crisis by a hasty and ill-considered action, and that there has been serious provocation. I am not suggesting that we should take it lying down. We have got to stand up for our rights—but let us show more wisdom than they have done. Already the public is generally sympathetic towards us on this matter, in spite of misrepresentation of the issue. If we can keep and increase this public sympathy, we shall win the dispute almost without a fight. The way to do this, I think, is to make a clear and definite statement of our case, and to ensure that it gets the widest publicity. Let us make it plain that we entirely reject the ——'s statement ; but in the first instance, at least, let us put our side of the matter in a sensible and reasoned way. If we do this I think we shall win the case, uphold the authority of the Union, and retain public sympathy all at the same time. If we can achieve this, it will be a sure guarantee against any future crisis of this sort.

I therefore propose that we should now (follow with details of proposals, stating points to be made and procedure to be followed).

THE STAFF

Hints.—This toast is proposed by one of the Directors. It should include an expression of the work done by the staff, and emphasis on the importance of teamwork. Any hint of patronage or condescension must be carefully avoided, but the speaker must not go to the other extreme and try to force over-familiarity.

SPECIMEN

Ladies and Gentlemen,—It is my privilege and pleasure to propose the health of the staff. The reason why it is a pleasure is that I welcome the opportunity to say a few things that I think every day. Whether work is a positive source of enjoyment, or merely a necessary evil, is a matter of opinion—personally I think it is a mixture of both ; but there can be no doubt that it is a good deal more pleasant—or, if you like, a good deal less unpleasant—if it is done in a spirit of mutual co-operation. We have that spirit here in a very high degree. I hope we shall always keep it.

Now I am not going to make a high-sounding speech about working for the honour and glory of the Firm.

This is a business house, and we are in business to make money ; and you work in the Firm with the same primary object. But, as you have shown, there is no reason why even the sordid job of making money should not be made pleasant ; and the way to make it pleasant is to work as a team. Teamwork means loyalty, and I know that no staff could be more loyal. I want you to know that your loyalty is appreciated.

I have talked enough. Ladies and gentlemen, I propose the health of the staff, and I couple with this toast the name of our old friend—old in service, but young in spirit—Mr. ——.

PRESENTATION SPEECH ON THE OCCASION OF A RETIRING EMPLOYEE

Hints.—In the specimen it is assumed that the employee is retiring on reaching the age limit. With very little alteration the speech can be made to serve where an employee is leaving for health reasons or to take another post. The speech must, of course, be generous in praise ; but on this sort of occasion the praise tends often to be overdone, with the result that the remarks lose their value.

SPECIMEN

Ladies and Gentlemen,—On an occasion such as this our feelings are bound to be mixed. Mr. Smith is leaving us today after thirty years' continuous service with the firm, to enjoy a well-deserved retirement. He takes with him our earnest wishes for his continued health and happiness for many years to come. No one would begrudge Mr. Smith the rest he has earned after his years of hard and selfless work ; yet we cannot pretend that we are happy to see him leave us. I do not want to say much about his value to the Firm, because that is a matter of which we shall be reminded, often painfully, for a long time to come. No one is indispensable, but there are some people it is very difficult to do without, as I fear we are shortly going to discover. We are going to miss our Production Manager—but much more are we going to miss Mr. Smith, the man.

As is natural in an organization of this kind, our respective relationships with Mr. Smith have varied a good deal. To some he has been one of the bosses, to be addressed as " Sir." Others have known him just as " Mr. Smith." To others again, he has been simply " Smith ;" and to a few intimate colleagues he has been plain " Jack." But his attitude to us has never reflected these differences. He has treated us all with the same unfailing courtesy and good humour. He has never been one to smile at the Directors and scowl at the junior clerks—indeed, from my personal experience he has inclined rather to smiling at the juniors and scowling at the Directors! By his cheerfulness and natural friendliness Mr. Smith has earned the respect of every one of us, and it is with a sense of real loss that we see him go. On behalf of the staff, I have the great pleasure of presenting Mr. Smith with this small token of our esteem and affection. This is a good-bye present, but I hope he will come to see us at times as a friend—if only to look in and gloat. Mr. Smith.

REPLY TO A FAREWELL PRESENTATION

Hints.—The presentation speech will in some measure govern the reply ; but it should be simple, quiet, and, above all, sincere.

SPECIMEN

Ladies and Gentlemen,—There is an Eastern proverb that says, " In the hum of the market there is money, but under the cherry tree there is rest." Well, I have been in the hum of the market for a good long time. There is a cherry tree in my garden, and it is to my garden that I intend to retire—I did not say rest !

It is difficult for me to realize that today I am leaving this firm where I have worked for so many years. I shall, I think, be quite happy without my work—and, in spite of Mr. Jones's kind words, I have not the slightest doubt that the work will get along very well without me. I was going to say that I have been only a cog in the machine, but I think a happier and more accurate description would be a member of a team. The small part I have played in this team has been made easy for me by the loyal co-operation I have always received from every other member. And it is the thought of leaving this team that makes parting so difficult for me.

Now my innings has come to an end, but I shall watch the future achievements of the team from a seat in the pavilion. You have given me a splendid souvenir to take with me, and I shall always prize this gift and what it stands for. Thank you for your kind present and especially for the kind wishes that have come with it—and good luck to you all!

USEFUL QUOTATIONS

Lost, yesterday, somewhere between sunrise and sunset, two golden hours, each set with sixty diamond minutes. No reward offered, for they are gone for ever.

—*Horace Mann*.

THE PRESS

Hints.—Very often the speaker begins by making a few mildly critical remarks about the Press, just for fun, and then retracts them as his speech continues. This sort of treatment is suitable for an able and experienced speaker, but the novice is advised to play safe and leave out the criticisms.

SPECIMEN

Gentlemen,—From time to time one picks up a newspaper and reads a letter from an irate reader complaining about some item, and solemnly informing the Editor that although he has been a regular reader for the·last forty years he will never buy the paper again. I often wonder if these correspondents carry out their threats, or if they get over their annoyance ; for on several occasions I have had the same feeling— not with only one paper, but with almost every paper I have read. One reason that I have got over my annoyance in the end is simply the fact that newspapers print such letters. Indeed, the correspondent has only to end

up by saying, " Of course you won't dare to print this,"
to make absolutely sure of seeing his name in print.

This, I think, is typical of one of the outstanding
virtues of our newspapers. They are fearless. Of course
they give the public what it wants, because a newspaper has got to sell ; but they do not shirk from giving
unpalatable news and making unpopular comments
when these are thought necessary.

Most of our newspapers are to some extent partisan,
and it is a fact that if you read the leading article of
two opposing papers on the same day you may get a
very different impression of the way the Government
is doing its job. But broadly speaking our newspapers
keep the opinions to the leaders, and do not mix them
up with the simple reporting of the news. The reader
can ignore the leaders if he likes. But it is most
important that they should appear, and the fact that
they differ from one another to such an extent is an
excellent sign of the health of the Press as a whole. In
some countries you will find that all the newspapers
express the same opinions. This makes things much
simpler for the readers, of course, but it means that
the Press is not free. For it is in the nature of things
for different people to hold different views, and the
free expression of conflicting views is precisely what
we mean by liberty and democracy. When I read two
or three conflicting leaders I am sometimes puzzled ;
but if I ever find that all the leaders are saying the
same thing, I shall be seriously alarmed.

It is sometimes said that the Press moulds public
opinion. Now I do not think that the representatives

of the Press who are with us tonight will take it amiss if I express the view that it would be nearer the truth to say that public opinion moulds the Press. If a citizen has a grievance, if he sees injustice in any department of our social life, his first thought is usually to write to the Press. You all know how many important issues have first come to light as a result of letters of this kind. You all know how many times the responsible authority has had to redress an injustice as a result of the publicity given to it in the Press. But what none of us knows is how many injustices and abuses of office do *not* occur because of the existence of a watchful and fearless Press. I suspect they are numerous, and for this reason above all the freedom of our Press must be held sacred. For the freedom of the Press is a guarantee of our own freedom.

Gentlemen, I ask you to drink to the Press and the health of its representatives who are with us tonight, and I couple with this toast the name of Mr. ——.

USEFUL QUOTATIONS

Four hostile newspapers are to be feared more than a thousand bayonets.—*Napoleon.*

With just enough learning to misquote.
                              —*Lord Byron.*

Amicably if they can, violently if they must.
                              —*De Quincey.*

It is easier to be critical than correct.—*Disraeli.*

Newspapers are the schoolmasters of the common people.—*Beecher.*

In these times we fight for ideas, and newspapers are our fortresses.—*Heine.*

Newspapers always excite curiosity. No one ever lays one down without a feeling of disappointment.

—*Charles Lamb.*

VOTE OF THANKS TO A LECTURER

Hints.—It is difficult to give general advice on this speech, for its contents and style will depend very largely on the subject of the lecture that has been given. For example, a vote of thanks to a Professor of Archæology who has lectured on Roman Britain would be entirely different from a vote of thanks to a professional cricketer who has given a talk on spin bowling. The following specimen, which is a vote of thanks to a temperance lecturer, must therefore be regarded as typical only to a limited extent.

SPECIMEN

Ladies and Gentlemen,—I am sure I am speaking on behalf of the whole audience when I say that Mr. —— has given us a remarkably instructive, lucid, and interesting talk. In my experience lectures on this subject all too often rely on sentimental and emotional appeals. Mr. —— has certainly not neglected the human aspect of his theme, and indeed he has drawn a vivid and graphic picture of the social and moral effects of alcoholism ; but he has placed his case on hard facts, and he has marshalled these in a way that to me, at any rate, makes them completely irrefutable. His arguments were entirely free from bigotry and narrow-minded prejudice, and the evidence he has brought forward is as conclusive as it is startling. I am convinced that no one can leave this hall without having been deeply affected by this lecture—for it is talks of this kind that can do more than anything else to combat the evils of drink. It remains for me only to propose a very hearty vote of thanks to Mr. —— for his admirable lecture.

USEFUL QUOTATIONS

Alcohol—liquid madness sold at 10d. the quartern.
—*Carlyle*.

If abstinence on the part of a temperate drinker would reclaim any drunkard, a man of ordinary humanity would practise it as far as considerations of enjoyment were concerned.—*Lord Bramwell*.

O thou invisible spirit of wine! if thou hast no name to be known by, let us call thee devil.—*Shakespeare*.

VOTE OF THANKS TO AN AMATEUR DRAMATIC SOCIETY

Hints.—This speech is usually made after a performance by the Society. It should be brief, and the speaker should be careful not to single out individual actors and actresses. The speech should always include a generous tribute to the work of the people behind the scenes.

SPECIMEN

Ladies and Gentlemen,—On behalf of the audience I should like to thank you all for the wonderful show you have given us. We expected it to be good, for we know how enthusiastic you have been in preparing for it ; but I am sure that none of us expected the production to be of this high standard. I only wish that some of the London critics had come here and seen what can be done by amateurs who combine enthusiasm and ability in such a high degree.

I am not going to praise any of the cast singly, because if I did that I should in honesty be bound to praise every one of you. You all played your parts superbly. But I hope you will forgive me if I do single out a few members of your Society for special mention. They are not on the stage, and indeed we have not seen them ; but we have seen the results of their work behind the scenes, and it would be impossible to praise this too highly.

When I add that I wish the Society every success in the future I am merely saying that I hope you will soon have another show ready for our delight. Again, on behalf of the audience, thank you very much.

IN AID OF CHARITY

Hints.—This speech will obviously depend to a great extent on the particular charity involved ; but the specimen has been made on general lines, so that most of it will be of use for almost any occasion of this kind.

SPECIMEN

Ladies and Gentlemen.—There is an unfortunate danger today in the idea that charity appeals are out of date and unnecessary. We have a Welfare State. In theory, we are all provided for from the cradle to the grave. The hospitals, and indeed the whole health service, are financed by compulsory insurance and taxation. Unemployment relief, public assistance, and pensions are similarly provided. It is easy—fatally easy—to conclude from this that charity is no longer necessary.

Of course charity is no longer necessary as it was. Of course there are fewer charities in the country. No one is going to regret this. But there still are charities, because there still are good causes that do not come within the framework of the national welfare scheme. The charity that I am asking you to support today is one of these. I do not think anyone will doubt that it is a good cause ; and it is a definite fact that it cannot continue to exist without private assistance.

In theory it should be easier to obtain this assistance now that there are fewer charities ; but in fact the reverse is the case. Partly this is because people are too ready to think that charities are no longer necessary, and partly because the State schemes have to be financed by all of us, including those who formerly gave voluntarily to charities. The subscriptions that we receive today are less than they were, and our costs have greatly increased. You know that nothing is wasted on administrative expenses—indeed, a very large part of the work is done voluntarily. Those who do this work are making their contribution, and a very valuable one it is. I ask you to make yours. However small it is, it will be a great help ; and I do not think you will ever regret having given it.